CONTENTS

AS LONG AS I LIVE

THOUGHTS ON GROWING OLDER

Jacob D. Eppinga

AS LONG AS I LIVE

THOUGHTS ON GROWING OLDER

Jacob D. Eppinga

CRC Publications
Grand Rapids, Michigan

ACKNOWLEDGMENTS

Text photos by William Lemke/Panoramic Images

Unless otherwise indicated, the Scriptures in this book are from the Holy Bible, New International Version, copyright 1973, 1978, 1984, International Bible Society. Used by permission of Zondervan Bible Publishers.

Printed in the United States of America on recycled paper. ⊕

Library of Congress Cataloging-in-Publication Data
Eppinga, Jacob D.
As long as I live: thoughts on growing older / Jacob D. Eppinga.
    p.   cm.
    ISBN 1-56212-052-2
    1. Aging—Meditations. 2. Aged—Religious life. 3. Aged—Conduct of life. 4. Eppinga, Jacob D. I. Title.
    BV4580.E66 1992
    248.8'5—dc20 93-35806
     CIP

10 9 8 7 6 5 4 3 2 1

Hello

There is a time for everything.
　　　　　　　—Ecclesiastes 3:1

here is a time to be born and a time to discover the world around us. Robert Louis Stevenson captured a child's wonderment when he wrote:

> The world is filled
> 　　with a number of things.
> I think we should all
> 　　be as happy as kings.

But time flies. Adolescence, the strength of youth, the middle years— these all pass by so swiftly. At the end is a time to die.

In the normal span of life, there is also a time before a time to die. It's called "Old Age," or "The Retirement Years," or even "The Golden Years," which often aren't really so golden.

Robert Browning wrote:

Grow old along with me.
The best is yet to be.

Some read these words and say, "Baloney—the best is gone when you are old." Art Linkletter used the saying *Old Age Is Not for Sissies* as a title for a book. Many can say "Amen" to that.

Some people describe the evening of life as the "over the hill" period. Among the ones who have gone over that hill are those who have stopped living, or, at least, have stopped living on the growing edge of life. They have given up. They are the men and women who mournfully refer to Ecclesiastes 12 as they talk about their aches and pains.

But as Yogi Berra, a former baseball great, once said about a game of baseball, "It ain't over till it's over." So, too, the Christian can speak of the game of life. We should be playing that game as hard in the ninth inning as in the first.

Zechariah, the priest and father of John the Baptist, said it well in his song. He praised the Lord who enabled him to serve without fear, in holiness and righteousness, *all my life* (Luke 1:75).

The psalmist wrote, "I will sing to the Lord *all my life;* I will sing praise to my God *as long as I live* (Ps. 104:33). Psalm 146:2 expresses the same thought in almost the same words. The Revised Standard Version has a slightly different rendering: "I will sing praises to my God *while I have being,*" which means while I am still here.

I am still here. So are you. Someone has said that those who are from sixty-five to seventy-five years of age are junior senior citizens. Those from seventy-five to eighty-five are middlers. Those over eighty-five are senior senior citizens. Being in the second classification qualifies me for visiting, via these pages, with all those who, like me, are in the time before the time to die.

Those who are under sixty-five may listen in if they wish.

The musings which follow are based on

    . . . reflections,
    . . . observations,

. . . some general reading, with a few specific nudges from two Dutch authors, C. A. Korevaar and G. Gilhuis,

. . . quite a few prayers that the pages ahead will prove helpful to others, and

. . . a heart filled with thanksgiving to "Anne" who has put up with me for over fifty years.

1

ARE OUR
SENIOR YEARS A BANE
OR A BLESSING?

Remember your Creator in the days of your youth, before the days of trouble come and the years approach when you will say, "I find no pleasure in them."

—Ecclesiastes 12:1

BANE

Some people say that Ecclesiastes is the most depressing book they have ever read. They say Solomon wrote about love when he was young (Song of Solomon); about wisdom when he was in his prime (Proverbs); and about gloom and doom when he was old (Ecclesiastes). Not all agree, however, that Solomon wrote the book. And some biblical scholars insist that Ecclesiastes doesn't even belong in the Bible. Martin Luther didn't include it in his Old Testament.

There's no universal agreement either about how one must read and understand this fascinating book. Some scholars maintain it represents a dialogue—similar to large portions of the book of Job—and that, therefore, not everything in it must be viewed as coming from the mouth of God.

I suppose Ecclesiastes will always remain a bit of a riddle. This is not to say we question its authenticity. The Belgic Confession identifies this book as "holy and canonical, for the regulating, founding, and establishing of our faith" (Article 5).

In Ecclesiastes 12 we find poetic reference to many an ache and pain that come to those of us whose middles are broader than our minds used to be. We chuckle knowledgeably when we hear the saying, "Everybody wants to get old but nobody wants to be old." As someone said to me upon reaching his three-score-and-ten, "From here, it's all downhill." Ecclesiastes 12 would seem to agree. Let's take a look at it together.

Verse 1:
Remember your Creator in the days of your youth, before the days of trouble come and the

years approach when you will say, "I find no pleasure in them."

It is important to remember that Ecclesiastes 12:1-7, although sometimes called "the Song of Age," is addressed to the young. It purposely emphasizes the negative side of age in order to impress upon the coming generation that its faith should be firmly in place before the trials of age descend upon it. Wise Solomon! Was he perhaps writing out of his own experience with aging bones? He tells young people that if their faith is going to hold them up tomorrow when the days of trouble come, they will have to root it firmly today.

Verse 2:
Before the sun and the light and the moon and the stars grow dark, and the clouds return after the rain.

Verse 2 likens old age to a dreary day or a dreary landscape. The rain may stop but never for long. No sooner are we over one hurdle but another looms ahead. There is always something!

Verse 3:
When the keepers of the house tremble.

"Keepers of the house" poetically refers to our hands. They are not as steady as they used to be. Have you noticed?

Verse 3 continued:
And the strong men stoop.

When we are old, our legs aren't as strong as they used to be. Ball players say the legs are the first to go. Have you noticed how we walk more carefully? We are not so sure-footed anymore, and elevators are a blessing.

Verse 3 continued:
When the grinders cease because they are few.

Modern-day dentistry has come a long way, and we all benefit. Even so, as one man said to me, "When I sink my teeth into a steak, they stay there."

Verse 3 continued:
And those looking through the windows grow dim.

Most of us wear glasses. Not a few of us develop cataracts. Night driving is more difficult. We are thankful for large-print Bibles; the print in my regular Bible kept getting smaller. The late, legendary Jack Benny (remember him?) said he didn't need glasses except for seeing, and they were cheaper than a seeing-eye dog.

Verse 4:
When the doors to the street are closed.

The "doors" are our ears. Deafness afflicts quite a few of us, and hearing aids are costly. One man bought an invisible pair. His family thought he couldn't hear, but he could. What he heard prompted him to change his will. Three times!

Verse 4 continued:
And the sound of grinding fades.

Here, the literal reference to a mill in its quieter moments is believed to be a metaphor for the voice, which loses strength as we age.

Verse 4 continued:
When men rise up at the sound of the birds.

Now that we are older, we do not sleep as soundly as when we were young. The early morning chirping outside our bedroom windows is more apt to waken us than it does our grandchildren.

Verse 4 continued:
But all their [own] songs grow faint.

I heard a choir of senior citizens. They were better than I expected them to be, but they were no Vienna Boys Choir. Some aging soloists ought to know when to retire. Oldsters have more difficulty reaching the high notes. They are not, generally speaking, so great on the lower ones either.

Verse 5:
When men are afraid of heights.

It's called acrophobia. Older folks don't like steps and stairs. We prefer everything on one floor. As a preacher, I find a pulpit is high enough.

Verse 5 continued:
And of dangers in the streets.

Unlike the young people's club in church, the senior society doesn't plan any roller skating parties. The older we get the more apprehensive we become. Old people shuffle and wield canes.

Pushcarts in supermarkets are welcome—we use them as walkers.

Verse 5 continued:
When the almond tree blossoms.

Our hair turns gray and then white. In Eastern cultures the first gray hair is hailed. It signifies the coming of wisdom. But in Western society it is pulled out or dyed.

Verse 5 continued:
And the grasshopper drags himself along.

Like the grasshoppers we drag ourselves on aging knees. If they are bad enough, we can have an arthroscopy or even total knee replacement. Oh, the marvels of this age! Even so, there comes a time when our knees buckle (and our belts won't).

Verse 5 continued:
And desire no longer is stirred.

With age comes a faltering interest in life. More specifically the reference here is to one's sexual drive which diminishes greatly from such heights of passion as find expression in Solomon's "Song of Songs."

Verse 5 continued:
Then man goes to his eternal home.

The changes of age culminate in death.

Verse 5 continued:
And mourners go about the streets.

The funeral procession.

Verse 6:
Remember him—before the silver cord is severed, or the golden bowl is broken.

The teacher says again, "Remember your Creator" (see verse 1). He likens life to a silver cord and golden bowl. This bit of poetic expression translates: life is precious, as silver and gold.

Verse 6 continued:
Before the pitcher is shattered at the spring, or the wheel broken at the well.

The poetic simile is now changed from life as precious as silver and gold to life as precious as a liquid which is spilled.

Verse 7:
And the dust returns to the ground it came from, and the spirit returns to God who gave it.

Remembering the principle that Scripture interprets itself, we must read this verse in the light of the great resurrection chapter, 1 Corinthians 15.

Verse 8:

"'Meaningless! Meaningless!' says the teacher. 'Everything is meaningless.'"

These words, a repetition of the book's opening verses, bring Ecclesiastes full circle. The writer uses a poetic device to end back at the beginning. However, we cannot conclude from this verse that life or old age is meaningless. Again, reading Scripture in the light of Scripture, we know this is not the Bible's point of view. As observed earlier, Ecclesiastes is a difficult book. Its dialogic character adds to the complexities of interpretation. But the author is not as negative as this verse implies. Notice the conclusion that follows verse 8 in which we are urged to fear God and keep his commandments.

I have seasoned the foregoing commentary with some light touches so some of us will not get too depressed. All of us who are the youth of yesteryear could add to the list of woes found in Ecclesiastes 12.

In fact, many of us do. Aching joints and cholesterol levels are high on our conversational agendas. In pastoral calls I have often listened to repeated recitals of physical burdens. One aged saint, long since gone to glory, was almost proud that she had eleven diseases—all of them fatal—including her "bronicals" (bronchial tubes).

The Bible is not blind to the ravages of time on our physical bodies. Indeed, it speaks in wonderment of a Moses whose eyes were not weak nor his strength gone despite his age (Deut. 4:7). At the same time the Bible is an honest book. It depicts us, warts and all, not only spiritually but physically too. Ecclesiastes 12 looks life full in the face and states black on white what happens to our bodies when we become old.

But there is another side. The Bible is never simplistic. If it speaks to us about predestination, it turns the coin over and speaks of human responsibility. It shows us that we are saved by faith and not by works so that no one can boast (Eph. 2:8, 9). But it turns this coin over as well to show us that faith without works is dead (James 2:17).

The Bible deals similarly with the subject of age. If it says on one page that old age is the "pits" (one man's explanation of Ecclesiastes 12), it tells us on another how beautiful old age can be (Prov. 16:31). These are not contradictions but truths—all of which must be understood in the light of each other.

Having seen some of the minuses of old age, let us also take a brief look at how the Bible shows us the other side of the coin.

Are Our Senior Years a Bane or a Blessing?

He has made everything beautiful in its time.

—Ecclesiastes 3:11

Are Our Senior Years a Bane or a Blessing?

BLESSING

Most of us have been "through it," as we say. The Great Depression of the thirties, World Wars I and II, and subsequent conflicts. Many of us have known illness, pain, and the loss of loved ones. Furthermore, we have all lived through a revolution brought on by civilization's unbelievable progress.

We were born into a simpler world. As children we never heard of computers, which, today, our grandchildren can operate. Many people now have jobs that didn't exist when we were small, and many that did exist then (remember the ice man?) are gone. The world we will leave bears little resemblance to the one we entered.

When we get together, we talk about other changes too. We consider the decline of morality. We ask, "Is the church going downhill as well?" We talk about the "good old days." There is even a magazine some of us subscribe to with that expression as its title, implying that these days are worse. When using an expression like the "good old days," we must remember it is a characteristic one, uttered throughout the generations by all those in their upper years.

The "good old days" can also be understood more literally to mean the good days now that we are old. Age brings perspective and ripeness. It is not correct to assume, as we do in this youth-oriented society, that the young have all the advantages. Other cultures seem more ready to grasp this fact. As I have already cited, gray hair is hailed and honored in other places.

Ecclesiastes 3:11 states, "He has made everything beautiful in its time." Many centuries ago the Lord said that "as long as the earth endures, seedtime and harvest, cold and heat, summer and winter, day and night will never cease" (Gen. 8:22). Those of us who have been around for awhile can testify to the truth of these words. We have seen many seasons come and go in their order and in yearly cycles. All have their own kind of beauty and appeal.

There is spectacular spring. How exciting to see nature come to life. Spring-time green is like no other green. But summer is lovely too. We sing, "In the good old summertime." Summer means long, lazy days, open windows, sunshine, soft rain, and lingering light at eventide. But fall, when nature's brush paints splashes of color on its forests, is gorgeous as well. Exciting spring, wonderful summer, spectacular fall.

And then there is winter. Many senior citizens seek to escape it. Even so, it has a charm all its own. It touches our imaginations and makes eloquent our praise. What is so lovely as a winter-scape, sun glistening on freshly fallen snow? Truly, when it comes to the seasons, God has made each one beautiful in its time.

As are the seasons of the years, so are the seasons of life. Here, too, are spring, summer, fall, and winter. The winter of life has rewards and beauties peculiarly its own, although we tend to see the negative side. We make jokes about the winter of life:

- Now that I know my way around, I don't feel like going.

- My forehead is getting higher, and my energy is getting lower.

- It takes me longer now to rest than to get tired.

- I have reached the age when I have to prove that I'm just as good as I never was.

It is healthy to joke about these things. But it is even healthier and better to see how the Lord makes everything, even old age, beautiful in its time.

I was struck by this fact a number of years ago. I was in my thirties. She was in her nineties. On one of my visits I asked her a searching question. Which decade in her life did she consider the best? I thought she might answer her twenties, when she bore children and could tuck them in at night. I would not have been surprised if she had said her thirties, when the children were growing in exciting ways. She could have said her forties, when, freed from earlier chores, she had more time for her

husband and her church. Or she might
have chosen her fifties, when she discovered the joys of becoming a grandmother. Imagine my surprise when she
chose her nineties as the best decade of
her life.

I offered a mild protest. Now that
she was in her nineties, she was less
able to get around. She was more
dependent on others. She might soon
have to move out of her house. "Surely,"
I said, "these years can't be your best.
Not as good as your twenties!"

I have never forgotten her answer. It
took me by surprise and made me
think. She said she had been so busy all
her life. But now, in her nineties, limited, and, as she put it, "out of circula-
tion," she had more time to pray. She
showed me her prayer list. I counted
over forty names. That list took up most
of her morning in prayer time. She
brought each one of her children and
grandchildren and a number of her
dearest friends to the throne of God
each day.

Many years ago, I read an old-fashioned book entitled, *Beautiful Old Age*. I
didn't understand it very well. Today, I

would understand it better. Indeed, I think I have—ever since my visit with that beautiful old lady who was so thankful for her nineties, which brought her more time for prayer.

Age brings other rewards. I have offered only one example. The teacher adds another in Ecclesiastes 3:13. He says we can enjoy the good of all our labor because it is a gift of God.

Because God made everything beautiful in its time, we must try to find the sweetness in our lives just as we try to find the sweetness in our food. Instead of waiting only for the joy of heaven, we should give thanks for the joy in our Lord, which we have even now. We should not waste the sunshine. As for the shadows of our winter's day, they will fade when brought into the presence of the One who is our light.

And so—our senior years.

Bane or blessing?

Life is what we make it.

Old age too. Let's talk about that in the next section. But first, let us reflect awhile.

REFLECTIONS

Are Our Senior Years a Bane or a Blessing?

- God told Abraham that he would be buried at a good old age (Gen. 15:15). What is a good old age?

  Pharaoh asked Jacob, " 'How old are you?' " (Gen. 47:8). Jacob replied, " 'The years of my pilgrimage are a hundred and thirty. My years have been few and difficult, and they do not equal the years of the pilgrimage of my fathers' " (Gen. 47:9). Based on his answer, what sort of an old man do you think Jacob was?

- Two of my parishioners were discussing the death of a third. "That's how I want to go," said the one, "quick!" The other disagreed. He wanted a good old age followed by a deathbed to which he would be able to call his children. He wanted the opportunity to point them one more time to the One who is the way, the truth, and the life. Having overheard the conversation, I wondered which view was best. Both of these men lived into their eighties, but neither got his wish. The one who wanted to go "quick" had a lingering illness.

The one who hoped he could have a fatherly farewell with his loved ones got his wish only in part. He did have a deathbed, but, having Alzheimer's, he knew no one. I buried them both. At a good old age?

- The fifth commandment (Ex. 20:12; Deut. 5:16) is the first commandment with promise. It will go well with those who obey it, and they will enjoy long life on the earth (Eph. 6:2, 3). What about those who obey the fifth commandment but do not receive the promise? I think about little Anne, an unusually sweet and obedient child, who died at the age of nine. One answer to the problem is to understand the fifth commandment's promise as addressed to the whole nation. A people who honor their elders have a future. Would you say that the Jews' elevation of the fifth commandment (strong family units) has anything to do with their enduring identity?

- Other passages in the Bible describe old age in terms of reward. Proverbs 3:1 is an example. Note the Psalms and their expressions of the blessings of age: Psalms 91:16; 92:14, 15. Read Psalm 128, which speaks of the blessing of seeing grandchildren.

- Consider Isaiah 65:20 where infants do not die and where those who do not reach 100 are accursed. How do you understand this passage?

2

ARE WE GROWING OLD
OR GROWING UP?

The glory of young men is their strength,
gray hair the splendor of the old.

—Proverbs 20:29

THE SPLENDOR OF AGE

I was making a pastoral call on a member who had just entered a rest home. As we were speaking, I glanced at the gentleman in the other bed. I thought I recognized him. After a more searching look, I was sure I did. Forty years before we had served together as fellow officers in a church. I had not seen him since.

I walked over to his bed to greet him and identify myself. I was struck with how he had aged. His hair and teeth were gone; his cheeks were sunken, and his skin was sallow. When I nudged him gently, his eyes opened but did not focus. Repeating my name, I leaned in closer and nudged him again. As I did so, I was even more impressed with how the years had taken their toll. Seldom had I seen one upon whom the aging process had left such a devastating stamp. Just then, he opened his eyes. I could see recognition dawn. Lifting his head weakly from the pillow, he mentioned my name. Searching my face, he said, "Boy, did you get old!"

Strange, isn't it? We see the aging process in others but not in ourselves. Weren't you surprised the first time you were called grandpa or grandma on the street? I know I was. The young hot rodder whizzed angrily past me on the road. I had been going five miles over the speed limit, so what was the problem? When I caught up with him at the red light, he leaned his head out the window and yelled at me, "You got to move it, gramps." I think it was the "gramps" part that irritated me the most.

Have you noticed how some younger people begin to treat us as if we are children? Isn't it really laughable when some believe all we can play is bingo?

So we strike back. Instead of acting our age, we try to keep up with the younger set. Although their legs should remain hidden, old men blossom forth in short pants (I thought we got rid of those years ago). At times old women aren't much better. You've heard the story, I suppose, about the young man who chased a blond down the street? When he caught up with her, he discovered she was his own grandmother!

Everything grows old: trees, dogs, cars—and us. John Milton wrote, "Time is the subtle thief of youth." Although the aging process begins when we are young, we don't notice it for a long time. In our forties or fifties we find that our children have surpassed us in strength. Soon there are other telltale signs: we develop liver spots on the backs of our hands; we cannot do the things we once did.

Ultimately, we reach sixty-fifth birthdays, the time to retire. For the traditional couple retirement means the wife loses her freedom during the day because she constantly has her husband underfoot.

Of course, sixty-five is a completely artificial milestone. Some years ago, Bismarck designated this age for the beginning of pension payments. He was smart. At the time most people didn't live that long. Those who did, didn't live much longer. Nevertheless, sometime in our sixth decade many of us begin to notice that our telephone lists contain a growing number of names followed by M.D.

When Pharaoh asked Jacob his age (Gen. 47:8), he was not being impolite. To be of great age was honorable in that culture. In our world it is otherwise. And so some lie about their age. The only way to tell a woman's age, they say, is in a whisper.

When we grow old enough, however, we often become less secretive. Some of us, who hated to reveal our age in the past, even begin to stretch the truth. A man of seventy-nine may tell others he is in his eightieth year. He tells it proudly, like the little girl who wants the world to know on her birthday that she is already seven.

Those in their seventies or older may even ask others to guess their age—often a mistake. They can be wounded when people guess they are older than they actually are. On the other hand, most people will be wary and purposely underestimate the number of years. How sweet it is to have others peg you at sixty-nine when you are actually seventy-nine. And how wonderful when children tell their mother she looks ten years younger than her younger sister.

In the company of oldsters, we often think of ourselves as the youngest—in age or spirit, or both. I remember attending a church service in Florida. The congregation was filled with snowbirds, not a child to be seen. When the minister called the little ones forward for the children's moment, none came. I whispered to my wife that we should get up. I said, "We're the youngest ones here." My wife indicated I should behave myself. I did, and it was probably a good thing. No doubt, the fellow ahead of me, who looked older, was actually younger!

In the previously quoted Genesis passage, Jacob told Pharaoh that he was 130 and that those years were difficult and not equal to the years of his fathers. Considering the strain he had been under, we should forgive Jacob's dour reply. He had not always been so negative. There had been a time when he had preened, flexed his muscles, and, singlehandedly, rolled a great stone away from the mouth of a well in the presence of the beautiful Rachel (Gen. 29:10). But when he stood before the great Pharaoh, he was a picture of age, defeat, and dejection. Life can do that to us if we allow it.

Proverbs 20:29 tells us that the glory of young men is their strength (as young Jacob at the well), but the verse goes on to say that gray hairs are the splendor of the old. And the splendor of the old is equal to the glory of the young. Only the old know something about God's patience. Only the old know something about God's long-suffering nature. That God had dealt with Jacob for 130 years was a miracle of grace. That God allows us to be here threescore-years-and-ten or fourscore years is also a miracle of grace. It is a miracle of love that God takes time to hone us. It is a miracle of mercy that he gives us time so we may grow in grace and in the knowledge of his son (2 Pet. 3:18).

These are the beliefs that can shine forth from the eyes of older Christians. Hanging on my study wall is that famous picture of an aged man saying grace. His gnarled hands are folded in prayer over a piece of bread and a glass of water. His old face is filled with that splendor of which Solomon writes and which comes to the devout Christian as the years mount and the skin wrinkles.

Time takes its toll. But it can also bring with it a deeper peace with God. For this to happen we need to mature in spirit.

Let's talk about that.

Teach us to number our days . . .
that we may gain a heart of wisdom.
—Psalm 90:5

THE MATURITY OF AGE

The splendor of age we talked about in the last section doesn't come automatically. We must work at it. Peter's final words in his last letter are that we must grow in grace and in the knowledge of our Lord and Savior Jesus Christ (2 Pet. 3:18). That's not easy.

Spiritual growth is not like physical growth. When we grow spiritually, most of us grow like acorns into oaks. Unlike the mythical creatures who sprang full-grown from the foreheads of the gods, our spiritual growth does not occur overnight.

Alexander Whyte, great preacher in Edinburgh, Scotland, once said that the victorious Christian life is a series of new beginnings. We have all experienced that in our lifetimes. We make a little spiritual progress. The devil knocks us down, and we have to start all over again. Whyte also observed that we would all like to take one giant step and immediately become archangels of purity. But sanctification doesn't happen that way. It is a long, slow process.

In Leviticus 19:32 God's people are told to rise in the presence of the aged and show respect for the elderly. In 1 Timothy 5:17 we read that the elders are worthy of double honor. It is an honor and respect, however, that must be merited.

A television comedian, whose popularity has waned, had the following punch line: "I get no respect." To paraphrase a popular television advertisement, to get respect, we have to get it the old-fashioned way—we have to earn it.

The same is true of spiritual wealth. Grace is free, but the fruits of the Spirit require cultivation and nurture (Gal. 5). That's work. The psalmist says, "So teach us to number our days." Work is implied in those words as well.

The story of Rehoboam is a sad one (1 Kings 12). He exchanged the counsel of experience for the advice of inexperience. He listened to his contemporaries rather than to his elders and, thereby, lost more than half his kingdom. This story, however, does not illustrate the superiority of age over youth. Old age does not guarantee wisdom.

The Bible presents many examples of unwise old age. The aged high priest Eli was a poor parent to Hophni and Phineas (1 Sam. 2). In his old age Solomon allowed his many wives to lead him astray (1 Kings 11:3). He indicts himself when he says in Ecclesiastes 4:13, "Better a poor but wise youth than an old but foolish king who no longer knows how to take warning." And Job observes how God silences the lips of trusted advisors (Job 12:20).

As age does not guarantee wisdom, it also does not automatically bring sanctification. That, says Proverbs 16:31, is only attained by way of a righteous life.

In this context older Christians sometimes nurse secret guilt. Years ago an older man confided in me. He had a secret sorrow. He had always been too busy to serve as an elder or deacon in his church. He declined each time he was asked permission to place his name in nomination. He said he would be happy to serve when he retired. But when retirement came, his health did not permit him to assume any office in the church. His refusals when he was physically able were a source of deep sorrow to him until the day he died.

Another man, an octogenarian, once told me a little verse was his daily prayer:

> Sins of youth remember not
> Nor my trespasses record,
> Let not mercy be forgot,
> For thy goodness sake, O Lord.

He sang this versified form of Psalm 25:7 out of his beloved *Psalter Hymnal*.

Shakespeare's guilt-stricken Macbeth asked the doctor:

> Canst thou not minister to a mind
>   diseased,
> Pluck from the memory a rooted
>   sorrow,
> Raze out the written troubles of the
>   brain
> And with some sweet oblivious
>   antidote

Cleanse the stuffed bosom of that
    perilous stuff,
Which weighs upon the brain?

The doctor answered, "Therein the
patient must minister to himself"
(*Macbeth*, Act V, sc. 3). As patients dis-
eased with sin and guilt, we, too, must
minister to ourselves with the help of
God.

Paul writes about becoming mature,
about attaining to the whole measure of
the fullness of Christ (Eph. 3:13). Such
perfection is only reached after gaining
the heavenly portals. Those of us coming closer to those portals feel we are
not as mature as we ought to be—and
could be. We feel we ought to be much
farther along the avenue of sanctification. We have not lived up to our potential in Christ.

Indeed, some of us often feel we
have retrogressed. I remember an aged
parishioner I served as pastor when I
was in my middle years. She not only
looked like a saint, she was one. I knew,
of course, that the only way any of us
will receive eternal life is through the
grace of God. We do not merit our salvation. Even so, I felt the day she died

the gates of heaven would be flung open wide to receive her. Her presence among us was like a benediction. She breathed the grace of the Lord Jesus Christ, the love of God, and the fellowship of the Holy Spirit.

Imagine my surprise when I found her greatly distressed in the rest home to which she had been moved and where she spent the last two weeks of her life. She had lost all her spiritual poise and security. She was totally lacking in that blessed assurance that had always been with her. I found her condition disconcerting, not only pastorally but personally. If she was so far from God, where did that leave me?

Just before she died, the peace of God again filled her. She repeated words she had often heard in church when I pronounced the assurance of pardon: "If we confess our sins, he is faithful and just and will forgive us our sins and purify us from all unrighteousness" (1 John 1:9).

What had happened to her in those disquieting days as she approached the gates of heaven? Satan was making one last-ditch effort to snatch her soul. The disciple Peter is not the only one Satan has desired to sift as wheat (Luke 22:31). He wants us all. This is one reason senior citizens of the kingdom often find themselves in spiritual crisis. Satan doubles his efforts to capture them before they are forever beyond his reach.

Earlier, I spoke about the other side of the coin. Remember? So here, too, I must turn it over. True, we all rue our lack of spiritual growth. Because we are new creatures in Christ by God's grace, there should be evidence of spiritual growth in us, which others, including our children and grandchildren, are able to see.

Perhaps you know the story of the man who held sermons in low regard. He said to a friend, "What good are they? I've been hearing them for fifty years, and I can't remember a single one." His friend responded, "I've been eating my wife's cooking for fifty years, and I can't remember most of the meals. But they have nourished me for half a century."

So it is with us. The Lord has nourished us for many years. Some of us have heard over 5,000 sermons. We have read the Bible or heard it read over 15,000 times. We have uttered or heard at least 20,000 prayers.

After all of that, how can some be so negative? I used to call on a certain parishioner every month. It was not one of my more pleasant tasks. Each time he reeled off his list of complaints—his children paid little attention to him; his wife was dead; his eyesight was failing; his life was past. This parishioner's litany reminded me of the prophet Elijah telling the Lord he had had it (1 Kings 19:4).

A healthy and mature old age is possible for Christians despite the trials and vicissitudes of life. A good description of healthy age is found in Psalm 92:12-15:

The righteous will flourish like a
palm tree,
they will grow like a cedar of
Lebanon;
planted in the house of the Lord,
they will flourish in the courts of
our God.
They will still bear fruit in old age,
they will stay fresh and green,
proclaiming, "The Lord is upright;

he is my Rock, and there is no wickedness in him."

To bear fruit in old age means we must stay on the growing edge of spiritual life. When I retired, my church gave me a pension. But God did not. I must continue to number my days that I may grow in wisdom, in grace, and in the knowledge of my Savior. So must you. We must do this as long as we live.

REFLECTIONS

- Some who are younger try to look older, but when they are older, they try to look younger. In some cases psychologists say the latter effort is a form of denial, a refusal to recognize the marks of the years. Vain old men dash around like Jehu (2 Kings 9:20) in loud-colored sportscars with tops down. Avoiding the rocking chair is good, but is there another side to this? Aging actresses, according to one Hollywood critic, try to look like "sweet young things." What is normal in this respect? What does it mean to "act your age"?

- I learned in catechism class that the process of sanctification is never complete in this life. There are those who disagree. Some branches of the church teach that perfection is attainable in this life. One can reach a level where one no longer sins. Is there biblical warrant for this position? 1 John 2:1a says, "My dear children, I write this to you so that you will not sin." Consider the rest of the chapter as well. Is there a tension between

1 John 2:1a, on the one hand, and 1 John 1:8 and Romans 3:10f, on the other hand?

- Opposed to those who believe in man's perfectibility are those devout people who lack assurance of their salvation. They are hesitant to partake of holy communion; they feel they do not have the spiritual maturity needed to approach the Lord's table. Their outlook, even in old age, is somber and heavy. What can be said for their point of view?

- In contrast, far more approach the table of the Lord in a casual manner. What about this attitude?

- In Genesis 25:8 we read that Abraham was "full of years." Some understand this to mean that he had had his fill of life and was ready to let it go. This is probably not the correct understanding of this verse, but is it a mark of progress in sanctification to be less desirous of life? In a hymn to the Holy Spirit, we sing:

  Spirit of God, dwell thou within my
      heart,
  Wean it from earth.

- Is it a sign of being grown-up in the faith when we are other-worldly and no more this-worldly, when we are heavenly-minded and not earthly-minded? If we are old and still very attached to this life, is this a sign of having grown old but not up?

Are We Growing Old or Growing Up?

3

CAN OUR LOSSES
BE TURNED INTO GAINS?

I have become like a bird alone on a roof.
—Psalm 102:7

LOSSES

Someone has said that the six ages of humanity are:

1. Beef broth
2. Ground steak
3. Sirloin
4. Filet Mignon
5. Ground steak
6. Beef broth

The late Bernard Baruch reduced the number to three:

1. Youth
2. Middle age
3. "My, you're looking well today!"

Another also agreed the stages were three in number:

1. You believe in Santa Claus
2. You play Santa Claus
3. You look like Santa Claus

I'm sure there are other depictions, but they have one thing in common. All show life as a toboggan run. It's all downhill, and the longer it lasts, the faster it goes. Some people find this slide extremely depressing. To counteract the realities of aging, they practice denial.

Some feel despair.

- Guy de Maupassant wrote, "I saw the awful loneliness of age coming, the short comings, no one near me, everything finished! Ah, there is my revolver."

- The philosopher Sartre wrote a story about a woman of thirty-six who had a relationship with a man of twenty. When the young man replaced her with a younger woman, the thirty-six-year-old, feeling her attractiveness diminished, committed suicide.

- I've read a play in which two old people, a father and mother, are each in a garbage can with only their faces showing. When they die, the lids come down.

- My friend is sorry he saw the movie *Amadeus*, the story of Mozart. "All I can remember of it," he said, "is the end when Mozart's body is unceremoniously dumped into a hole in the ground. It haunts me."

A questionnaire was circulated in a retirement home. It asked, "When did you first find yourself growing old?" The answers varied, yet all questionnaires revealed that people reckoned age more by losses than by years. Some said, "When I had to give up my house and come here." Others replied, "When I quit working"; "When our youngest left home"; "When my partner died"; "When I had to give up driving the car."

When was the first time some loss made you think about your age? Was it the loss of sight, hearing, hair, or teeth? Was it the time when a young lady stood up to let you have her seat on the bus? That's not easy for men who have always opened doors or given place to the ladies. How long since you have kept a magnifying glass handy? Or increased the wattage in your reading lamp? Or bought a hearing aid or a cane? We used to rest when we were tired. But then we were "up and at 'em" again. After we rest now, we are often still tired. We used to bounce back after an illness. Now it takes us longer to recover, and we never quite do.

Not only do *we* reckon our age in terms of losses, others do too. They ask, "Are you going to travel alone—how brave of you!" Apparently, we are perceived as no longer at our peak.

The nurse speaks to us as if we are children. "When you have finished, leave your sample in the room. The cup has your name on it. Then come out, cross the hall, and go to room seven. The number is on the door. It's down the hall to your left. Not your right. In room seven there is a chair for you. Sit on it and leave the door open. The doctor will see you there. Remember, room seven."

Our losses are not only physical. Besides not being able to remember names, other changes occur. We no longer have the same attitude towards those birthdays, which keep coming. We don't anticipate trips like we used to. Packing bags and sleeping in strange hotels always sparked feelings of adventure. But now the glow of these things, if not altogether gone, has surely lessened. Of course, grandchildren are a great joy. Frankly, however, it would be very difficult if we had to rear children all over again. We wouldn't be up to it, either physically or mentally.

We experience a loss of a different kind that is more spiritual. As we grow more careful walking down the street, so, too, we tend to grow more conservative walking down the road of life. Seeing how our children live makes some of us wonder what young people are coming to! And we wonder—are things going in the right direction in society and in the church? We become concerned. But when we get together with others who are also concerned, we notice that all heads in the group are gray.

The loss of a job because of retirement is, for some, a time of crisis. When we visit our workplace soon after our first pension check, we find that all are happy to see us. We must share the coffee break. The next time, the welcome is still cordial. It doesn't take long, however, before a feeling of estrangement sets in. Furthermore, the work seems to be going on very well without us. Some of us retire and become consultants, but we are never consulted. Suddenly, we feel superfluous. We are unneeded. This loss of place in the scheme of things can bring an inner crisis. We couldn't be missed. Now we are expendable. They couldn't do without us. Now, they don't even remember to send us a Christmas card.

Some homemakers find greater difficulty adjusting to new roles than men and women retiring from the workforce. There was a time when mother was in constant demand. It was always "mother this and mother that." Neither the children nor her husband could do without her. But now that the children have "flown the coop," there is a void. Some homemakers then feel their lives lack purpose.

The list of losses due to aging is not a short one. In addition to those already cited, there is the loss of friends. "I know more people in heaven than on earth," said an old man to me as he stared out of his rest home window. A crushing loss is that of one's life partner, a burden more women bear than men.

Such losses often result in loneliness and boredom. It is understandable that loneliness and affliction are mentioned in the same breath in Psalm 25:16. I have become "like a bird alone on a roof," cries the psalmist in Psalm 102:7.

Boredom is as devastating as loneliness. It begins in the morning hours. It stares with empty eyes at the television screen. Its companion, idleness, is the devil's tool. And so for some older folk, disillusionment sets in. They consider their lot in life and ask, "Is this all there is?"

They echo the teacher in Ecclesiastes 1:8 who says, "All things are wearisome." They have read stories to their grandchildren in which all lived happily ever after. But these are fairy tales. Reality is otherwise. It is easy, in such a mood, to enter the portals of depression. Thinking about past failures and even successes, about what might have been or could have been, digs them deeper into the pit into which they are descending.

Losses have a cumulative and devastating effect on the human spirit. Those mentioned come in whole or in part to all of us. Together, they spell the loss of youth. In another age or culture this loss might be less poignant. But in our society age makes many feel they no longer belong.

Consider, for example, that in our world today sport is king. Speaking to a confirmation class of young people, Albert Schweitzer urged them always to go to church and never to allow sports to usurp the day of worship. But sports have taken over our Sundays, and the rest of the week as well. Our gods are sports figures. Our heroes are not the faithful homemakers or breadwinners but those who have set the newest athletic records. Millions are paid to those who are best at playing squat tag, or whatever. In such a sport-dominated world you are old and out of it sooner rather than later.

Consider, too, that in our world sex is king. Sex is today's great occupation and preoccupation. A person must have sex appeal. Razor blades, automobiles, and everything in between are sold via ads in newspapers and television screens by beautiful young women revealingly undressed. In a sex-dominated world you are, again, old and out of it sooner rather than later.

We also live in a world where technology is king, bringing almost daily changes. Older people accommodate themselves less easily to change—automation, credit cards, computers, money machines for deposit and take out, the list goes on and on. Many older people simply cannot handle all the paperwork which is their lot simply because they have gone to see the doctor. In a world of increasing technology the old find it difficult to cope.

Another effect of the loss of youthfulness is the loss of confidence. When we were young, we barged ahead where angels feared to tread. We married, had a family, bought a house. We took a risk and started a business. Today we wouldn't dare; one of the marks of age is the loss of confidence.

This loss brings worry. Will I be able to meet my bills? Will Social Security be cut? Will my pension disappear? Shall I sell my house and move into a retirement home? Do I have enough saved for an emergency? How long will I live? How will I manage?

The fear of death, to which I have referred in passing, also arises. How many other fears and concerns are hidden by the aged, as this one so often is? It is difficult to show others our concerns in a world in which the unwritten rule is that we must put up a good front.

Have I taxed your attention long enough on the subject of losses? Let me mention one more before I end the list. It is the loss of opportunity. We had so many plans and goals. We were still going to do so much. We had dreams, but we ran out of time. We made some mistakes, and we were going to correct them. We were going to start a new business, take a new direction, get some project off the ground. But, suddenly, we discovered we were too old, and it was too late. Remember the man I mentioned who was going to take an active part in the work of his church some-day? When he was finally ready to do so, it was too late. The infirmity of age had robbed him of the opportunity.

Some of us remember the Great Depression of the 1930s and the stock market crash of 1929. The financial losses were incalculable. But there are other, even more serious, kinds of losses. Old age brings them into focus. Young people cannot know them. But we have become acquainted with many of them.

Is there anything we can do about them?

Let us see.

*"I will pour out my spirit on all people.
Your sons and daughters will prophesy,
your old men will dream dreams, your
young men will see visions."*

—Joel 2:28

GAINS

I was only a boy, but I still remember
the sign in the restaurant:

As you go through life, brother,
Whatever be your goal,
Keep your eye upon the doughnut,
And not upon the hole.

I cannot say that I have always followed that good advice. When I did, I
learned something. When you keep
your eye on the doughnut, the doughnut looks bigger, and the hole looks
smaller. When I didn't observe the
maxim, I learned something too. Then
the hole looked bigger and the doughnut, smaller.

We have been concentrating for a
few pages on the hole in the doughnut—the losses we experience when we
are older. In doing so, the more we men-

tioned, the bigger they seemed. That's the way it is. Some people dwell on the negatives of old age, and so those negatives are magnified.

Someone has defined socialized medicine as old people getting together socially and talking about their aches and pains. Some call it an "organ recital." I like the senior citizens group where, I am told, you pay a fine each time you mention one of your ailments. It is good when we are discouraged from complaining and good when we discourage others too. The next time someone asks, "Did I tell you about my operation?", answer by saying, "No, and I appreciate it."

Various hints can help the aged place their losses in proper perspective, hints worth their weight in gold. One is that we must take care of our bodies as best we can. Stay fit as a fiddle, it is said, and you won't end up looking like a bass viol. Of course, we all have our individual shapes and sizes. People vary a lot more in this respect than, say, horses. We can do something about our shapes, however, particularly if we are prone to overeat—an easy thing to do in retirement. There are enough restaurants around to make it possible for us to go to a different one each day of the week for a year. Furthermore, modern advertising whets the appetite. But in a world in which we know more about proper diet than ever before, it is our Christian duty to avail ourselves of the knowledge the Lord has made available to us in his providence, and thus, to eat sanely and exercise moderately.

Another helpful hint towards keeping proper perspective is to accept our wrinkles. We may even take justifiable pride in them and tell others we earned them. It is much easier on our psyches and also our purses or wallets to go with the flow. Age can have a beauty all its own. There is nothing wrong with going to a beauty parlor so that we may look our best. On the other hand, there are limits. People who spend small fortunes on beauticians' fees might well ask themselves whether their expenditures are justifiable in this world of so much need.

I knew a man who told me his wife spent hours with mirrors and makeup before going out to dinner. I read that the late Mae West would not appear in public when she was old unless the lighting was right. Others submit to repeated face lifts. And some, like the late Greta Garbo, go into seclusion rather than have others see what the years have done.

All of this is very tragic. Indeed, such behavior merely accentuates the negatives. It is much easier, even more moral, to take the view that wrinkles bring character and be done with it.

It is also good to develop some deafness as to what others may be saying. When the long-lost friend in the rest home looked at me and said, "Boy, did you get old," God gave me the grace and sense of humor to laugh about it. Indeed, it was laughable to hear him say to me what I had been thinking about him.

In England these words are chiseled in stone: "People say. Let them say." In 1 Corinthians 4:3 Paul says, "I care very little if I am judged by you or by any human court." He goes on to say the Lord judges him.

There is a sense in which it is right to be impervious to the judgments others make of you. Someone asked an aged saint, "How does it feel to be over the hill?" The old man could have been affronted by the insensitivity. Instead, he smiled and said, "The view is splendid."

Senior citizens should also remember how God has used older people. Moses was one hundred twenty, and God used him mightily. Some scholars say that Paul was well over fifty before he began his first missionary journey. Ronald Reagan was president of the United States in his seventies. Douglas McArthur was supreme commander in his seventies. Thomas Edison started a chemical plant in his sixties. Kant wrote his *Anthropology* when he was seventy-four. Verdi composed *Othello* at seventy-four and *Falstaff* at ninety. Titian painted a masterpiece at ninety-eight.

Of course, these are accomplishments of extraordinary people at unusual ages. To mention them almost does a disservice to the many senior citizens who have been such a blessing to others in smaller ways. If all oldsters were removed, the world would be greatly impoverished. The mix of young and old is a divine blend in which both elements exist for mutual benefit.

To ensure mutual benefit, the older generation should give the next generation room to expand, grow, and develop in its own way. To tell the young that yesterday was better helps neither them nor us. To say that our ways were better only aggravates them while reminding us that we are no longer in the saddle.

This does not mean we have to think like the younger generation. If you are tempted to do this in matters where your convictions are at stake, then, by all means, hold on to your standards. For example, it has become acceptable in today's society for some people to live together without benefit of clergy. We have no need to accommodate ourselves to that perspective. If it was wrong when we were young, it is still wrong today. We live in a changing world. But that doesn't mean we have to accept or approve of all changes that have occurred.

The most important suggestion I can give to the old is this: we must live out our days with God's Word in our hands and hearts. The Bible is a book we do

Can Our Losses Be Turned into Gains?

not outgrow. Indeed, we need it more than ever in our upper years. God's word is a lamp to our feet and a light upon our paths (Ps. 119:105).

When enumerating our losses, we dealt with the loss of opportunity. We had planned to do so much, but now it is too late. There are other things we ought to have done (Rom. 7). We have committed sins of omission and commission, and we cannot reverse the clock to erase them.

We all have these regrets, and we must seek forgiveness where it can be found (Ps. 130:4). But it is good to know that while we left so much undone, Jesus did not. For us he cried on the cross, " 'It is finished' " (John 19:30). Therefore, we can have the assurance, as Paul says, that he who began a good work in us will carry it to completion (Phil. 1:6), even though we feel we could have done and should have done so much more for him.

Meanwhile—to borrow a phrase from Q&A 111 of the Heidelberg Catechism—we should, even now towards the close of our lives, "work faithfully" for him.

We missed opportunities in the past. There was that cup of cold water we didn't bring. Some of us stood at the grave of a loved one and thought of things we should have said and done; now it is too late. I have conducted countless funerals and have seen the flowers that came too late. But there is one matter for which it is not too late, whatever our age, and that is to accept Christ as our Savior and Lord, if we have not done so. For even if we are a hundred, now is still the day of salvation.

In dealing with our losses, we mentioned the feeling, "Is this all?" It is here, too, that the gospel has the answer. I remember a man who complained he had not gotten much out of life. He had been dealt a poor hand, he said. And now it was almost over. Other people, he said with a sense of irony, win a million dollars from *Reader's Digest*. But, of course, something like that would never happen to him and never did. Having struggled to make ends meet all his days, he had become a little bitter, especially because he had seen so many of the wicked prosper (Ps. 73:3).

I could not help being sympathetic because, although never lazy, he had not had an easy lot in life. On the other hand, I had to tell him he was staring at a very small hole in the doughnut. He was doing it with a magnifying glass. After all, I said, God had given him a good wife and fine children. He was not poor. Above all, God had set him completely free (Heidelberg Catechism Q&A 18) and had given him an eternal inheritance (Heb. 9:15). What if he had gained the whole world and lost his soul? It would have been a bad bargain indeed.

"It was good," he said, "that you came." He had been feeling sorry for himself.

I said, "We all get that way sometimes." Little did he know I needed the medicine I brought very badly myself that day.

But what about that other sense of loss—the one we feel when we are no longer helping the world go around? We have been pensioned off. After the initial exhilaration of being retired wears away, we feel ourselves unneeded and worthless. It is good, then, to hear the Lord tell us the hairs of our heads are numbered, and, if he notices sparrows, he is certainly aware of us (Matt. 10:30-31).

In Job 8:8 Bildad the Shuhite says, " 'Ask the former generations and find out what their fathers learned.' " So don't feel so unnecessary. We have wisdom and experience to share with the following generations (Ps. 48:13). In Psalm 71:18 we read, "Even when I am old and gray, do not forsake me, O God, till I declare your power to the next generation, your might to all who are to come." We have a great responsibility to the next generation. Instead of feeling superfluous, we should know we are needed.

Other duties and responsibilities fall to us. People who are ill or lonely, or both, need a call, a card in the mail, or a helping hand. We also need to tend to our own continuing spiritual growth. " 'Let him who is holy continue to be holy' " (Rev. 22:11). And there is prayer. Remember that wonderful lady I told you about? She was in her nineties, yet she had very busy mornings because she had so many for whom she uttered a daily petition.

Missionaries often mention that they sensed the prayers of God's people back home. They felt the support. The great missionary Paul prayed for his supporters but asked for their prayers as well (Col. 1:3). In 1 Thessalonians 5:25 he says, "Pray for us." Praying for God's workers in the field is something we all can and must do.

Remember the song, "My Mother's Prayers Have Followed Me"? Many an errant child has been brought back to the family of God through such a faithful ministry.

Intercessory prayers and petitions, however, are not the only prayers to pray. We must remember our prayers of confession—we do not need to be convinced of their necessity—and our prayers of thanksgiving.

Above all, we must render our prayers of adoration. A man of God kneeled to pray as was his custom. Another, who was curious, concealed himself behind a door. He wanted to hear what the man of God uttered in his prayers. He listened. He heard, "O

Lord God, whom have I in heaven or earth but you?" (Ps. 73:25). The eavesdropper listened for what would follow. But all he heard was a repetition of what he had already heard. Nothing more. That man of prayer was St. Francis of Assisi. His prayer was only one of adoration.

In assessing our losses we spoke of the loss of activity that leads to boredom. We observed that it could become the devil's tool. We have already seen how Satan intensifies his attacks on the aging in order that he might snatch them, even at the last, from the hands of God. It is important, therefore, that we do not let our guard down but make sure we have the helmet of salvation and the sword of the Spirit—the Word of God (Eph. 6:17).

Oldsters as well as youngsters need to pray, "And lead us not into temptation" (Matt. 6:13). In answer to Question 127, the Heidelberg Catechism says that the devil, the world, and our own flesh never stop attacking us, and so we must "firmly resist our enemies." "Strengthen me according to your word," says the psalmist (Ps. 119:28).

Thus, old age is not the time to give up on Bible reading and study on the grounds that we have been exposed to the Bible all our lives. A seminary professor I served as pastor sold all his books. He had a severe illness, and his scholarly work was done. But each time I called on him I found him reading the one book he still had—his Bible.

The loss of friends and resultant loneliness can never approach the loneliness Jesus suffered for us in his life and on the cross where he was forsaken of the Father. He endured this loneliness so we might avoid it. As God the Father said to Joshua, so he says to us, "I will never leave you nor forsake you" (Josh. 1:5). At the close of the gospel of Matthew, God the Son says, "I am with you always, to the very end of the age" (Matt. 28:20). In John 14 Jesus said he would send the Holy Spirit to be with us forever (John 14:16).

And so on the deepest spiritual level the Christian cannot be alone and lonely because of the presence of the triune God. In the ninth article the Apostles' Creed also reminds us we have "the fellowship of the saints."

In dealing with our losses by focusing on our gains, we must also remember what Joel the prophet said. In his Pentecost sermon Peter quoted him: "Your old men will dream dreams" (Acts 2:17). Young and old will together see visions and dream dreams. There will be no generation gap. Instead, old and young will be a team. The old will not look down upon the young, and the young will not write off the old. This is what took place when the Spirit descended upon the church. And so it shall be in the kingdom.

Zechariah (8:4) shares Joel's vision. He writes, "This is what the Lord Almighty says: 'Once again men and women of ripe old age will sit in the streets of Jerusalem, each with cane in hand because of his age. The city streets will be filled with boys and girls playing there.'"

Malachi, the prophet, sees this same vision. The Old Testament closes with these words, "He will turn the hearts of the fathers to the children, and the hearts of the children to their fathers" (Mal. 4:6).

Thus, senior citizens, you have a role to fill.

I have mentioned many texts in the foregoing paragraphs to set the losses of age in their proper perspective. And so the Christian of threescore-years-and-ten and fourscore-years-or-more can see the retirement years not as a postlude but as an interlude. We are not at the end.

There is more to come.

Much more!

We are marching to Zion!

REFLECTIONS

- In this section we deal with Psalm 71. It is the only song in the book of Psalms in which the poet, presumably David, talks about the subject of his age. Try to find yourself in it. You may wish to identify the losses or gains of age which are found or implied in it. What follows is designed to stimulate your thinking on this beautiful psalm. It is possible you may discover some unexplored depths either in it or in yourself.

- This song has some repetition. Older people tend to repeat. Some of us tell our children the same story over and over. Are the repetitions in the psalm due to age, or are they for emphasis?

- Note the difference between Psalms 71 and 92. The latter refers to age in passing. Can you summarize the difference?

  Psalm 71 is a plea for support in old age. What special support does old age require?

- The references to the past in this psalm are not in the manner of one who recalls it as better. The past is

*Can Our Losses
Be Turned into
Gains?*

remembered, instead, as a cause for thanksgiving for God's faithfulness. We should do likewise.

- Psalm 71:1 is the same as Psalm 31:1. Is this plagiarism? If the author is the same, then it is not. Can we then conclude that this was a characteristic expression of David? If so, what does it reveal about his character?

- Psalm 71:1 was presumably written later than Psalm 31:1. There must be more experience behind Psalm 71:1. How wonderful to persist in earlier ways if they are right!

- Can Psalm 22:5 be taken as an answer to Psalm 71:1b?

- Could verses 2-4 of Psalm 71 refer to the Absalom insurrection? Some commentators think so. Others believe these words to be sufficiently vague for us to pour our own needs into them.

- In verse 5 of Psalm 71, we read, "Since my youth." David knew the Lord from birth. This blessing is all too often taken for granted by those who have been born into the covenant. Do you agree?

- Consider verse 9 of Psalm 71. Why was David distressed? Were past sins rising up before him as is often the case with older people? See Psalm 51. Those who have experienced the nearness of God will testify to the awfulness of his absence.

- Look at verse 14 of Psalm 71: "I will praise you more and more." This is the opposite of that growing self-centeredness evident in some older people. This will be touched on in a following section.

- In verse 17 of Psalm 71, we find repetition again. It hearkens back to verse 5. David, it seems, is so impressed with God's love for him since birth that he must sing of it again. This is beautiful!

- Does verse 18 of Psalm 71 reveal a deep yearning for a few more years in order that David may witness to his children and their generation? What is our reason for wanting a few more years?

4

CAN WORRY
ADD A SINGLE HOUR
TO OUR LIVES?

"Martha, Martha," the Lord answered, "You are worried and upset about many things."
—Luke 10:41

95 _____
*Can Worry Add
a Single Hour to
Our Lives?*

WORRY

Making monthly calls on aged shut-ins can be a blessed task. Usually, I found it so. When John celebrated his 100th birthday, we came with coffee and cake. On his 101st birthday he wasn't in his room. He had been brought outside where he could enjoy the sunshine. I found him on the balcony smoking his pipe. Pretending shock, I said, "You shouldn't be smoking. It will shorten your life." He smiled, extended his pipe, and said, "Here. Have a pull and lengthen yours."

He had a sense of humor, and age never dulled it. On his centennial when I asked him if he thought he would make the next hundred, he thought it was quite likely. He said, "I'm a lot stronger now than when I started the first hundred."

Ella was an equal delight. She was too naive to understand jokes, but she was always a ray of sunshine. She had had a hard life. Her late husband drank himself into the grave. She never had any children. She had done housework for others and taken in washing all her life. Nevertheless, she was always happy. The good fortunes of her friends were a particular delight. When I told her that my family and I were going to Florida for the first time, she seemed even more thrilled about it than I was, even though she had never been there herself. She squealed with happiness at the prospect of her pastor going there with his dear wife and dear children.

When I called on Mabel (names are fictitious), I always made sure to follow up with a call on Ella. That was because Mabel was always so depressing. Every month she subjected me to a litany of concerns. Mabel's world was filled with worries, and no assurances from God's Word seemed to dispel them.

The contrast between these two daughters of Zion was startling. Sometimes we wonder how brothers and sisters from the same nest, having had the same training, can be so different. It is the same with the family of God. Ella and Mabel were sisters in the Lord, but they did not resemble one another. Ella kept her eye on the doughnut and Mabel on the hole. Ella was the sunshine. Mabel saw all things through a glass darkly.

A little of Mabel is in most of us; the upper years bring the resemblance into greater focus. We read our newspapers more and our Bibles less. We worry about wars and rumors of wars. But that is not the whole of it—we worry about our health, our children, our possessions. Worry is one of the more prevalent sins.

Many of us worry about our health. I must confess I never did until my bout with cancer. Lying in the hospital at my lowest emotional ebb, I couldn't have been cheered even by Ella. It is not true, as some people say, that when you have your health, you have everything. If you have your health but not the Lord, you have nothing. Still, health is an immeasurable blessing, and ill health can be worrisome. There are those who, like John Calvin, can manage it, but for others ill health can be a source of great anxiety.

Some people worry as much about money. "It's easy not to worry about money," someone said, "when you have it." What that person didn't realize is that many people who have money worry about it more than those who don't have it. I remember an elderly, well-to-do gentleman who lived in a retirement home. More than once I found him sitting in his chair with his bankbooks, reviewing his balances.

Of course, when you don't have money, you have cause for concern. Especially when you are old. Some of us remember a famous poem, written in 1920 by Will Carston and entitled, "Over the Hill to the Poorhouse." It was about an old woman whose children wouldn't have her.

Over the hill to the poorhouse,
my children dear, goodbye!

Many a night I've watched you
  when only God was nigh,
And God'll judge between us.
  But I will always pray,
That you shall never suffer
  the half I do today.

Years ago, I had to take someone to
the county poor farm. We don't call
them poor houses and poor farms anymore. But as the Lord said, "The poor
you will always have with you" (Matt.
26:11). Indeed, in these days when there
is more rather than less poverty, more of
the aged find themselves in this catego-
ry. Meanwhile, expenses soar. The doctor
prescribes pills; the pills are so expensive. Escalating costs are not easily met
with thinning wallets and purses. Will
rent and taxes go up again? Is there no
end? Keeping an aging body and soul
together can bring sleepless nights.

A lot of us worry about the future.
Should we stay where we are? Is it time,
perhaps, to find a place with a nursing
facility attached? The house has
become too big now that the children
are gone. The upkeep is too much. It
would be good if we could live in a
home with no stairs. But can we afford

the retirement home, and, if so, will we like it? What will become of all the things we have, many of which are dear to us? We push the retirement-home thought away because there is no place like where we are. Home.

Still, we're not getting any younger! Eventually, we need to come to a decision—if the Lord tarries. But could we give up the privacy we now enjoy? It may not be much, but our home is our castle. In it we eat what and when we like and get up when we please. If we ever go to a "home," we have to observe eating hours. Will we like institutional food? Still, the longer we wait, the more expensive it will be. The rates go up all the time. But how can we make the move when making it seems so much like heading for the last round-up? And so we go—round and round—and worry.

Others of us have taken the plunge. We did it. It wasn't easy. Now we miss those pieces of furniture that were a part of us. I remember an octogenarian who moved into a "home." Indeed, it was I who had persuaded him. He went reluctantly. The next day he called me. "Get me out of here," he said. "There's nothing here but old people." I smiled. But I misunderstood. It wasn't that he didn't think of himself as old. What he meant was he missed the sounds of the children playing next door in his former neighborhood.

Happily, he settled down. So do many who finally make the move. But many others worried a lot before they made the leap. First came fear about making the decision. Fear led to anxiety. And fear and anxiety add up to worry.

I have discovered that another cause for great worry these days is the fear of Alzheimer's disease. Cancer is still a dreaded word; many feel they will get it in one form or another eventually. Yet there seems to be an even greater fear of losing one's mind. I don't know how many aging saints have said to me, "If I can only keep my mind!" It is a great source of worry.

It is amazing how many people secretly believe they already have the beginning stages of something dreadful. Many confuse their loss of a sharp memory with incipient Alzheimer's. "Pastor," they say, "I can't remember names anymore!" Or, "When I go to the refrigerator,

I don't always know whether I'm there to put something in or take something out." They seem little relieved when I tell them I have the same problem.

I tell them the story of the old man whose name I couldn't recall. When I asked the man his name, he stood before me for several seconds before he finally said, "How soon do you have to know?" My joke, however, brings little relief. I tell another joke—the one about the person who was always speaking of the hereafter. He goes to the refrigerator, or down into the basement, pauses and says, "What am I here after?" I get smiles for these stories but not very big ones. The fear is still there. The loss of mind is a deep worry. But too many of us worry about things that never happen.

This is not to say we should dismiss such concerns lightly or consider ourselves immune to mental disorder. To visit someone who tells the same story ten times in an afternoon or who says it's time for church when it's only Friday is a sobering experience. To visit a rest home and see those whose eyes are empty is not easy. Remember the man I told you about who hoped he would have a deathbed rather than a sudden departure, so he could point his children one last time to the Lord? Remember also that when he got his wish, he didn't recognize his family anymore? Remembering people like him makes it easy to understand why old people say to me, "One thing I pray for—that God will allow me to keep my mind as long as I live."

I pray this prayer too. Yet if I do lose my mind, I won't know it, unless perhaps in the initial onset. Floating back and forth through time, tending dolls, may be better than some other experiences that can befall us. I remember a lady I called on monthly. Earlier in life she had been the soul of hospitality. I could never leave her house without being served something. Now she was tied down in a wheelchair. However, she seemed oblivious to that fact. She invariably asked me to stay for tea and have a piece of delicious cake she had just baked.

Remember Ella, my ray of sunshine? At the end her mind, too, became enveloped with mysterious mist—she thought of me as her daddy. When I called on her, she wanted me to tell her stories. I was there when she died. I

Can Worry Add a Single Hour to Our Lives?

kissed her forehead and held her hand. She went peacefully because daddy was there. After I wiped my tears, I reminded myself that it was actually true. Her heavenly Father was there.

Sometimes, however, the fallen nature appears in those no longer in possession of their senses. They were always circumspect regarding the name of God. Now they curse. We are fearfully made, yet wonderfully too (Ps. 139:14). Truly, in age, perhaps more than any other time, we need to ask God to make us stouthearted (Ps. 138:3). And should we come to such a pass that we no longer know our own name, God does (Isa. 43:1). How wonderful!

Despite all our worry, our comfort is in knowing we belong to God in body and in soul, in life and in death (Heidelberg Catechism Q&A 1), and in age. Someone has observed that the Bible contains 365 "fear nots"—one for every day of the year. Reading those should help us dispel worry, for worry is an enemy. It reduces vitality. It impairs both reason and will. It has many of us in its grip.

I have not begun to list all the worries that furrow aged brows. Nor will I try. One I mentioned earlier in this book is the fear of death. Someone said to me, "I don't fear death, pastor. But how I will die is something that occupies my mind. When it gets to me, I tell myself that even if my death is a painful one, it can't be as bad as the death my Lord suffered for me."

Apparently, this was his way of handling worry about death. Others may have no fear. But it would be unfair of me to say we shouldn't have any concerns about when, where, or how we die. Death is unnatural. We were born to live. Death is an enemy. Although Jesus has conquered it, he nevertheless deals gently with our apprehensions. That's why so often he reassured us with these words, "Fear not."

So what must we older folks do with all the worries that come with age? We used to sing this old song:

> What's the use of worrying
> It never was worthwhile,
> So pack up your troubles in your old
>   kit bag,
> And smile, smile, smile.

Is this the way? There is a better way. To find it we must turn to the Lord.

Cast all your anxiety on him because he cares for you.

—1 Peter 5:7

Can Worry Add a Single Hour to Our Lives?

TRUST

In his *Letters to an American Lady* C. S. Lewis asks, "Do pious people in their reverence for the more radiantly divine element in Christ's sayings sometimes attend too little to their sheer, practical common sense?" The common sense of which C. S. Lewis speaks is surely found in these words of Jesus from the Sermon on the Mount, "Do not worry about tomorrow, for tomorrow will worry about itself. Each day has enough trouble of its own" (Matt. 6:34). The King James version of this passage has found its way into the English language as a proverb known to all: "Sufficient unto the day is the evil thereof."

The New International Version of this text sounds almost as if it might be found in the Almanac. Instead, it is in the Bible. The words sound like they might have appeared in Uncle Ned's column of advice. Instead, they come from Jesus himself. When age brings worries and fears, it is good for us oldsters to pay special attention to Jesus' words of sheer, practical common sense and apply them.

When Jesus tells us each day has enough trouble of its own, he is telling all, including senior citizens in the kingdom, that they must live one day at a time. This means, first of all, we should not live yesterday today. Memory is a wonderful thing. It can enrich old age. God often asks us to exercise our memory. He tells his people to remember the days of old. He tells young people to remember their Creator in the days of their youth. Holding bread and wine, Jesus says, "Do this in remembrance of me." The faculty of memory is a blessing. We would be immeasurably impoverished without it.

As God urges us to remember, however, he also teaches us to forget. Paul said, "One thing I do: forgetting what is behind and straining toward what is ahead" (Phil. 3:13). It seems, then, there

Can Worry Add a Single Hour to Our Lives?

are some things to remember and some things to forget. Wisdom is knowing which is which. It is precisely at this point that some of us run into trouble—we forget what we ought to remember and remember what we ought to forget.

Some of us remember our sins of the past. They may be a source of great worry. Years ago, I dealt with a man who, in his younger years, had repeatedly broken the third commandment. He had taken God's name in vain daily. He had long since rid himself of this sinful habit, but it was still causing him distress. He had taken his burden to the Lord, but he had never left it there. Another with whom I dealt was convinced he had committed the unpardonable sin. He had confessed, but he couldn't be pardoned. Both of these gentlemen were living their yesterdays. I tried to tell them if they had confessed their past sins, they should forget them. We need not remember what God has cast behind him (Isa. 38:17).

In the same vein, some of us need to forget yesterday's successes; they make it hard for others to live with us today. In all of this, we must practice a kind of mental, spiritual discipline with the prayer, "Lord, help me to remember what I must remember, and forget what I may forget."

George Herbert once said:

> Undress your soul at midnight as you do your body, shedding as you do your garments your sins of commission in prayer and penance, so that you will waken in the morning a free person with a new day.

Those who continue to live in the past are like the souls in Dante's *Inferno*, doomed to remember the past for all eternity. Like cows who endlessly chew the cud, chewing what has already been chewed, some older people continue to worry about what has already been forgiven.

In pondering the words of Christ enjoining us to live one day at a time, we must also remember he was exhorting us not to live tomorrow today either. It is true, we must live in faith and hope, two virtues which have focus in the future. Then, too, as Proverbs tells us, we must not be improvident with respect to the future. And yet Jesus does not want us to be so preoccupied with tomorrow that we cannot live in and enjoy the present.

But old habits are hard to break. Some of us have lived our whole lives putting up with the present because we couldn't wait for tomorrow. We couldn't wait to graduate from school. We couldn't wait to get married. We couldn't wait for the children to grow up. We couldn't wait for retirement. And we couldn't wait for somebody to die, so we could get the inheritance. Having developed the habit, we are still focusing on tomorrow, borrowing troubles that may never come, and worrying about them.

Jesus asked, " 'Who of you by worrying can add a single hour to his life?' " (Matt. 6:27). Has anyone ever added an inch to his height or in any other way controlled the future by worrying about it? For some of us, tomorrow never comes. We die first. The Bible says, "You do not even know what will happen tomorrow. What is your life? You are a mist that appears for a little while and then vanishes" (James 4:14).

Have you ever noticed how many of our generation sigh and ask, "What is the world coming to"? Perhaps you have asked the question yourself. If so, you are in good company. Perhaps you recognize all or some of the following names: Charles Colson, Malcolm Muggeridge, Carl Henry, Aleksandr Solzhenitsyn. This is the company you are in when you see the future darkly. Each man is a prophet with credentials. Each one sees our culture in decline. One sees us headed for the dark ages. Another sees us drifting towards neopaganism. Another traces with alarm the waning of the church in our Western world. Each says the same thing but in different ways.

After reading what these modern prophets have to say, we grow anxious and worried. When our grandchildren sit on our laps, we wonder what in the world they will experience in their lifetimes. We begin to worry about tomorrow, and in so doing, live tomorrow today.

If we are Christians, a blessed thought then comes to mind. The greatest prophet of all is Jesus. He is far greater than the few we have mentioned, but he is not in disagreement with them. Indeed, he paints an even worse future. He makes direct predictions concerning tomorrow. Although he predicts the tribulations that are to come, nevertheless, he says, "Do not worry about tomorrow."

A question arises in our minds. How can Jesus say this in view of the persecutions that are to come? But we know the answer: he who has the world in his hands also has tomorrow in his hands. Some older folk have time on their hands. He has time in his hands. And so, Christian, relax.

Note, however, that although we must not live yesterday or tomorrow today, we should live today today. Too many of us do not make constructive use of the limited time we have. A traveler in South Africa saw some children playing with stones. On closer inspection he discovered they were playing with diamonds, for he was in diamond country. We play with something more precious—time. To paraphrase Job (28:18), surely, its price is beyond rubies. Nevertheless, we play with time, waste it, or kill it.

Leisure time in retirement is a blessing. Sometimes we tell others we are busier now than we ever were. Perhaps some of us are, although, generally, we say it tongue-in-cheek. But those who fill their days with nothing or spend time only on themselves need to reconsider. There must be a reason for getting up in the morning. Our lives still need purpose. Playing golf six or seven days a week while giving no service to God or neighbor is not, I think, what Jesus has in mind for us when we go about our retirement years.

Can Worry Add a Single Hour to Our Lives?

How can we avoid worrying about the past or the future and concentrate on each day as it comes? We have discovered this is not easy. Yet we should observe the words of Matthew 6:34: "Therefore do not worry about tomorrow, for tomorrow will worry about itself. Each day has enough trouble of its own." And we should live with, lean on, and listen to the One who gives us these words.

A step in the AA (Alcoholics Anonymous) program can help us. AA never insists that a person sign a lifelong pledge of total abstinence. It simply encourages members to begin each day by resolving not to drink for twenty-four hours. AA knows not one member has the power to submit to such an agonizing discipline for even one day. And so AA says a member can only go successfully through one day by recognizing and leaning on a higher power.

Do Christians know this? It is really not possible to keep ourselves from living yesterday or tomorrow today. Yesterday burdens us with regrets, tomorrow with fears. And yet by trusting in Jesus, we discover the only one who can release us from guilt of the past, the only one who can relieve us from fear of the future, and the only one who can free us to live today today.

It is important, then, that we take Jesus at his word when he tells us not to worry. If we don't, he will come to us and ask, "Why do you call me Lord, Lord, and do not do what I say?" (Luke 6:46).

A number of years ago, an elderly woman asked to speak to me about her funeral. She said she was ready to die. Her illness was terminal. Paraphrasing 2 Kings 20:1, she said her house was in order. She had some requests regarding her memorial service. There had to be a message for her family and friends, especially her grandchildren. "I want you to speak very directly to my grandchildren," she said, "and remind them of grandmother's favorite hymn:

> Trust and obey, for there's no other way,
> To be happy in Jesus, but to trust and obey."

Shortly thereafter, she died. I honored her request when we came together to lay her body to rest. I reminded the grandchildren of grandmother's favorite hymn and told them to make it theirs. Then we sang it: "Trust and obey." This is the only way we can practice what Jesus preached in the Sermon on the Mount when he told us not to worry.

On occasion I have had to wait a few hours at the big airport in Chicago, one of the busiest in the world. I watched airplanes come down from the sky unendingly. Meanwhile, others were taking off, also unendingly. I wondered how those pilots taxiing to the end of the runway dared to roar into the sky. The truth, of course, is none of them dare. There is a control tower, and someone is in it. Furthermore, communication is possible between the pilot revving his motors and the man in the tower. It is only when the pilot is told he can take off that he does.

So it is with us. Free of worry, we can take off in life, even at our age, because there is someone in the tower—our Lord in heaven. He tells us to lift our wings, free from fear, and soar. The only way we can do so is to trust ourselves wholly to him and to what he says.

Remember those teams of horses on the streets when we were children? I remember such a team, hitched to a wagon and too frightened to move because of noisy model Ts coming down the road at breakneck speeds of up to thirty miles an hour. I remember a man climbing into the wagon, taking the reins, and making a clicking sound with his tongue. Then those horses, too terrified to move, moved.

So it is with us. The older we get, the more apprehensive we become about everything. Everything around us moves faster. We become afraid, and we worry. Then we sense that someone has reins on us. The hands that hold the reins bear the scars of nails. He whispers, "Fear not." He says, "Don't worry."

And so oldsters—in Christ, dare to live.

REFLECTIONS

- We have observed that there are things we must remember but also things we must forget. Wisdom is knowing which is which. Psalm 103 is pertinent here and makes for profitable reflection.

- Notice that David is talking to himself. He is getting a little older, and he is doing what many older folks do. My image in the mirror, for example, often prompts me to make a few unflattering remarks to myself. Did you ever talk to yourself while driving and notice others, at the red light, seeing your lips move? Of course, young people do this, too, but old people do it a lot. In Psalms 42, 43, 62, and in a few other places as well, you can find soliloquies—people talking to their souls.

- In Psalm 103 David reminds himself of something very important—the need to remember all his blessings. His memo to himself is in the second verse. In it David lays down the law to himself. He needed to do that, and so do we. In reviewing my pastoral experiences over the years, I am struck by the fact that so many of the kingdom's senior citizens have not forgotten past disasters. They say, "I remember the Wall Street disaster when people lost their money"; "I remember that awful time when the tornado struck"; "I remember the fire we had." There is nothing wrong with this. We cannot very well forget those disasters that happened. They will be with us to our dying day. But if we remember only bad experiences of the past, we may tarnish both ourselves and our witness in the present.

• David could easily have done the same and thus changed his song in Psalm 103 to a dirge. Plenty of disasters occurred in his past. Instead, he mentions some sins and diseases (verse 3), and in verse 4 he recalls when life was the "pits." But notice where he places the emphasis. He remembers such past benefits as forgiveness, healing (verse 3), and redemption (verse 4). The list goes on to include God's love and compassion, good things, and renewal (verses 4-6).

- Remember Ella? One day she said to me with glowing face, "Oh, I can't thank God enough!" Such also was the mood of David in Psalm 103. This should spur us to some self-examination.

- We have observed that trust is the cure for care. There is much to reflect on in this matter. Martin Luther said we cannot prevent the birds flying about our heads, but we can keep them from building nests in our hair. A good maxim for older folks.

- Are there some Bible references that have been helpful to you in your struggle against worry? One that has helped me is Philippians 4:6: "Do not be anxious about anything, but in everything, by prayer and petition, with thanksgiving, present your requests to God." In the light of this text, I have always pictured myself as a child with a tangled string. The first thing I did was go to my mother or father, whose patient fingers unraveled the worrisome snarl.

- We put our worldly affairs into hands of experts, and we are relieved. We commit our sickness into the hands of the physician, our broken cars into the hands of mechanics, and our business complications into the hands of lawyers. Generally, we go to them sooner rather than later and put our trust in them. Should we do less with the business of our souls? If we cast building cares into the hands of carpenters, surely, we should do the same with those things that weigh down our spirits—by going to our God.

Can Worry Add a Single Hour to Our Lives?

5

ARE WE GROWING OLD GRUMPILY AND NEGATIVELY OR GRACEFULLY AND POSITIVELY?

Teach the older men to be temperate, worthy of respect, self-controlled, and sound in faith, in love and in endurance. Likewise, teach the older women to be reverent in the way they live, not to be slanderers or addicted to much wine, but to teach what is good.

—Titus 2:2-3

NEGATIVE

When I was a boy, my parents raised canaries as a hobby. I remember seeing tiny creatures emerge from tiny eggs. It was a miracle. We went to buy canary seed and other supplies from a widow, who was in the business. She was very old and bent. She wore an ill-fitting jet-black wig that covered her forehead down to her eyebrows, the upper lines of a wrinkled, leathery face. Alas, the wig didn't quite make it in the back, where wisps of pure white hair were plainly visible.

126

*Are We Growing
Old Grumpily
and Negatively or
Gracefully and
Positively?*

We called her the bird-lady, not only because of her business but also because of her plumage. I loved to go to her place. The rooms of her house were filled with bird cages. All were occupied by canaries, parakeets, parrots, and other exotic feathered species I could not identify. No furniture was in sight. I wondered where she slept. I also wondered whether she imitated her parrots, or if her parrots imitated her. Her voice sounded more like theirs than that of a normal human being.

Nevertheless, I never missed an opportunity to accompany my father on his infrequent trips to the bird-lady on Bewick Street. It was such a delightful experience. Her house was filled—as she was filled—with song. She sang to us—"hello," "goodbye" and all words in between. And she sang to her birds who, in turn, sang back to her. She was far from a Jenny Lind. She sang like an old crow, if an old crow could sing. High above her song and that of the bigger birds, the canaries warbled up a storm. The whole house was filled with joyful music.

So, too, old age can be filled with music.

Remember Ella?

Softly, O softly, the years
   have swept by thee,
Touching thee lightly,
   with tenderest care,
Sorrow and pain
   did they often bring nigh thee,
Yet they have left thee
   but beauty to wear.

Are We Growing Old Grumpily and Negatively or Gracefully and Positively?

All old age, however, is not beautiful. All old people are not happy. When we only add years to our life and no life to our years, then our last season becomes the winter of our discontent. And so young people need to know how to live so their old age will be a melody, not a dirge.

It is possible, however, to live life in a major key and yet end the last years in a minor key. We speak of the sins of youth, but there are also sins of age. Many a man and woman have lived life on the growing edge. But retirement proved to be their undoing. Not handling it well, they became crotchety. Is old Solomon of Ecclesiastes the same person as young Solomon who wrote of love and middle-aged Solomon who blessed us with his wisdom in Proverbs? What happened to him? King Saul emerges in the Bible as a splendid young man. With such a son as wonderful Jonathan, Saul should be sitting on top of the world instead of skulking down some back alley to consult a witch. What happened to him?

Naomi was happy as a lark. She had two sons, which, in her culture, was a blessing from the Lord indeed. But when she came back to Bethlehem, back to the old neighborhood, the whole town wondered, "Can this be Naomi?" She did look older, but it was more than the crowsfeet on her face that had altered her appearance. People had not seen the dullness in her eyes before. She spoke to her old friends, " 'Don't call me Naomi,' she told them. 'Call me Mara because the Almighty has made my life very bitter' " (Ruth 1:20). She went on to speak of her affliction and misfortune.

Naomi had suffered the great loss of her husband and two sons. Such an experience is devastating. There are others, however, who have also been through deep waters who do not say, "Call me Mara," meaning bitterness. My friend Ella, bless her, was certainly a case in point. She, too, had gone through life's depths, but she ended up in old age with a heart as full of song as the bird-lady on Bewick Street.

129

*Are We Growing
Old Grumpily
and Negatively or
Gracefully and
Positively?*

What are some of the sins of age we oldsters need to avoid so we can live positive lives as long as we live? Surely, it is biblical to say that as long as we are here God wants us to avoid the negative stance. Many of us have sung a song, popular years ago:

> You gotta accentuate the positive
> Eliminate the negative.

That is good advice for all, including those whose hair, if any is left, has turned to silver. Paul told Titus there were some things older men and women had to learn (Titus 2:2-3). He told Titus to teach them. No doubt this was a difficult assignment. Teaching old dogs new tricks isn't easy. Getting them to break bad habits is well-nigh impossible. Even so, let us see what some of those bad habits, or sins, or mistakes are.

130

*Are We Growing
Old Grumpily
and Negatively or
Gracefully and
Positively?*

Self-esteem

First of all there is self-importance. Its opposite, a low self-image, is also on the list. We can treat them together. When I was a child, visiting clergy often stayed at our house when our pulpit was vacant—generally a good experience for me. Most of the ministers were pleasant to have around. I remember one exception: an older man who carried his dignity on his sleeve. In the evening he told my mother what he wanted for breakfast. He treated her as if she were the servant rather than the hostess. Little boys notice things like that. But he never noticed me. He overlooked me. As far as he was concerned, I didn't exist. He wore a winged collar above which bobbed his Adam's apple as he spoke endlessly at the table to my father. I had to sit still and couldn't go out to play because we had not yet prayed the closing prayer. To this day, whenever I meet older people bloated with self-esteem, I think of this man. Of course, younger folk can also have this flaw. But I am thinking more at the moment of the older ones who list all their accomplishments for us plebeians to admire.

The opposite, a low self-image, is not a positive trait either. So many of our children have surpassed us in education and accomplishments that we prize ourselves less than we ought. When our grandchildren operate computers that baffle us, listen to music that mystifies us, speak easily of famous names in the world of television, movies, and sports of which we never heard; some of us feel out of it and over the hill.

The constant proliferation of modern inventions leaves most of us farther and farther behind. We retreat and grow morose. Psychologists have identified this mood and named the causes. Falling farther behind in a world of whirl and speed causes some of us to drop out of the race gladly and altogether.

Egocentrism

Another negative, egocentrism, can result from those flaws already mentioned, although often its roots cannot be traced. It is a deadly pit in which to fall. There are those of us who make the world revolve around ourselves. Remember the shut-in I mentioned who, on my monthly visits, subjected me to her litany of ailments? She never tired of speaking about herself.

I am reminded of a joke: a certain man spoke endlessly about himself. Finally, he said to his friend, "But I have talked enough about myself. What do *you* think about me?"

Excessive self-concern is counter-productive. It makes us boring. People begin to avoid us. If all we speak about to others is ourselves, we soon lose our audience. This is especially true when we list our troubles. We soon discover that others will turn a deaf ear. It is too bad that people given to egocentrism do not have enemies bad enough or friends good enough to tell them their flaw. And so the rest of us must endure and endure.

> To sing in heaven with the saints
> above,
> Oh, that will be glory!
> To dwell with them on earth,
> That is another story!

Overdependence

Overdependence is another trap into which some of us fall. Generally, we prize our independence and hang on to it as long as we can. We don't want to move in with the children, and most of them appreciate it. In our society we live on wheels, and so we hold on to our cars, some of us longer than we should. We are thankful for social security and pensions and for the independence these afford. When we move into retirement homes, we feel we are giving up some of our independence. We find it difficult to be in the dining room at specified hours if we want to eat. Even so, such places do their best to recognize we need as much independence as possible.

On the other hand, some of us find ways to lean on our children. Even though they have their own lives to live, many have been prevented from doing so. I remember a woman who was the youngest in a family of eight children. Eventually, all the other children left, and the father died. The youngest daughter was left to care for her mother—something she was still doing at age

134

*Are We Growing
Old Grumpily
and Negatively or
Gracefully and
Positively?*

sixty when her mother was ninety. This was not because of the daughter's nobility of character. Although she loved her mother, her lot in life was thrust upon her, not only by her mother but by siblings as well.

I also remember a bachelor, who, according to his mother, was too good for any of the available young ladies. The mother died when her son was fifty, a time in his life when he felt it was too late for him to find a partner. A domineering and dependent mother caused his situation. I must confess I never had the nerve to hold a mirror to her face.

It is indeed a blessing when willing and loving children, nieces and nephews, are concerned for us older people, when children return to their parents that which they received from them. Such a blessing of caring children must not be abused.

Self-pity

Some older people wallow in self-pity. And sometimes it is excusable. An older man in a rest home was called on faithfully by his two children every

Christmas. That would have been commendable if they had lived on the other side of the world. But they lived in town. In this case I did have the nerve to speak to his children about their neglect. Alas, with unfavorable results. I was told to mind my own business. It would have been better if the old man had borne his sorrow in silence. Instead, anyone who spoke to him even briefly found him eliciting their pity.

I recall another situation involving an aged mother in a retirement village. Her only son lived far away in Florida. Each time I came to see her she told me her son down south had just called her on the telephone. Imagine my shock and surprise when I learned he had not called her in years. Such nobility—the opposite of self-pity—and all to cover her bleeding heart!

Self-pity can be brought on by character or circumstance or both: sorrow resulting from the loss of a dear one, ill health, failure in business "because somebody cheated me." Many causes give rise to sourness, cynicism, and self-pity. These things grow in the soul that feels sorrow for itself.

Hypercriticism

We need to guard against growing hypercritical in old age. It is a slide that too many of us enjoy. Think of all the things of which to disapprove. Have you seen the way some people dress these days for church? Our neighbor's boy has such long hair he looks like a girl! You hardly see any women in skirts anymore. The girl across the street looks just like a boy! Can you imagine—everybody in church is calling the minister by his first name! What is the world coming to?

Perhaps some of us need to talk less about what the world is coming to and more about who is coming to the world. It is less in his name and more in the name of custom that we criticize. I must confess to a similar impulse. I don't like it when parishioners call ministers by their first names in services of worship. A greater formality shows greater respect. I'm also not sold on people going to church in gardening clothes. I am prone to snort, "You wouldn't dress that way to meet the president or the prime minister!"

If we are not careful, hypercriticism can go to outrageous lengths. I have an acquaintance whose mother disapproves of her daughter's taste in clothes, wallpaper, friends—everything. This disapproval doesn't cement their relationship. It is not wrong to be critical of wrong things that matter, but even in such cases it is good to be circumspect lest we be classified as negative.

Retrospection

Closely allied to hypercriticism is retrospection. Some of us are prone to compare all things of today with those of yesterday. It is not good to live in the past, although it is understandable. Those were the days when we counted. We had jobs. We were factors in the scheme of things. We were recognized. It is easy to fantasize and make the past better than it was. That the good old days were not all that good in all respects doesn't register. Thus, some of us begin to tell others for the umpteenth time about how things used to be and who we were and what we did. But most people are not like the little boy who says, "Grandpa, tell me what it was like when you were young."

138

*Are We Growing
Old Grumpily
and Negatively or
Gracefully and
Positively?*

Conservatism

Conservatism is another trap into which some of us fall. It, too, is closely allied to hypercriticism. Conservatism, properly understood, is to be prized. I am a conservative in theology. I think that is good. But I also tend to be conservative about everything else—something that comes with age—and that is not always good. To do something a certain way because that's the way it was always done before is not a good reason. Change for the mere sake of change is also not good. But we must realize time does not stand still. To idolize old ways and hang on to them is a mistake.

Undeniably, to grow old and remain progressive is atypical and difficult. Some of us are too old to adapt to new ways and changes. But where wisdom accompanies age, there people will not be so set in their ways they will reject all things new.

You understand my list of negatives cannot be complete. The seven deadly sins—pride, envy, anger, sloth, avarice, gluttony, lust—might well be considered here, for age does not place us beyond the reach of any. I have touched on a few. Those not listed could easily be included. Even the last—lust—should not be overlooked. Enough have been mentioned, however, to alert us that there are sins of age; it is our Christian duty to strive against them. I mention one more.

Doubt

Earlier I spoke of an aged saint for whom, I thought, the doors of heaven would be flung wide open upon her death. To my surprise, her last days were filled with doubt. Satan had destroyed her assurance of salvation; not until the very last was it restored.

Others of us also harbor doubts. Some don't merely question their own faith but question whether the Bible is really true. Is salvation and the gospel which proclaims it nothing but a giant fairy tale after all? Is there a God? Is there a hereafter? For some these are the deepest and most private thoughts, shared with none.

140

*Are We Growing
Old Grumpily
and Negatively or
Gracefully and
Positively?*

There are reasons for such doubts. We have lived long enough to question Lord's Day 10 of the Heidelberg Catechism which deals with the doctrine of providence. Do all things really come not by chance but by way of a heavenly Father's will? What about that sweet little nine-year-old girl struck down by a brain tumor? What about that splendid young man with a wife and small children removed by cancer? With Asaph in Psalm 73, we wonder why the wicked prosper. The world gets worse and heaven is silent. Is Jesus really coming again? You'd think he would have come by now! The church is a disappointment. We can find as much goodness outside it as in it. These thoughts creep into our minds. We hide them in the darkest rooms and put a padlock on the door. Even so, they are there.

Sometimes we get the key, open the door, and look at them. In our youth we wrestled with doubts. In our middle years we were too busy. But now in old age, when the end is nearer, some of us wrestle with them again. We wonder whether our prayers rise higher than the ceiling. Our wrestling can lead to serious spiritual depression.

These, then, are some of the pitfalls into which we can fall in older years. Bishop William Culbertson, dean of Moody Bible Institute, was often heard to pray with his students, "Lord, help us to end well." This should be our prayer too. That prayer, however, needs to be accompanied by our sincere efforts to avoid all that which would cause us to end poorly. We need, as best we can and with God's help, to eliminate the negative.

141 —————

Are We Growing Old Grumpily and Negatively or Gracefully and Positively?

This is the day the Lord has made; let us rejoice and be glad in it.

—Psalm 118:24

Are We Growing Old Grumpily and Negatively or Gracefully and Positively?

POSITIVE

Over a decade ago I landed in the hospital where I remained for over eight weeks. The length of that stay, coupled with surgery and complications, contrived to lower me into a spiritual Grand Canyon. I turned my face to the wall and not to the Lord. "Why me?" I wondered. One sleepless night I reached for my radio to distract me from my pain. A distant station brought the voice of a hillbilly evangelist. His grammar was atrocious. Before I could turn him off, he began to play a hymn on a scratchy record:

Be not dismayed, whate'er betide,
God will take care of you.

The music quieted my inner turbulence. Indeed, before the record ended, I found myself singing softly along in my mind, personalizing the words:

God will take care of me.

I had switched from negative, at last, to positive. I ask your indulgence for this personal reference. I would avoid it except it makes a point. We can only be sick graciously or grow old graciously by remaining close to the Lord.

When I returned home at last, I thought the dandelion in our front lawn was the most beautiful flower I had ever seen. A text sprang to mind. "This is the day the Lord has made; I will rejoice and be glad in it." The spirit of thankfulness destroys the spirit of grumpiness that can mar our days.

I remember visiting a nursing home I had never been to before. An old parishioner had just moved in. I asked whether she liked the place. She said she did, but she had one complaint. An old man with a stentorian voice conducted evening devotions on the intercom. She said, "He thinks he can sing," indicating with a facial expression that he couldn't. As I left, I stopped at the office to speak with the supervisor. I

144

*Are We Growing
Old Grumpily
and Negatively or
Gracefully and
Positively?*

said the lady I had called on found the devotions on the intercom something less than edifying.

The supervisor smiled and said, "A retired minister. He's ninety—you should hear him."

Expressing a desire to meet him, I went with the supervisor to the retired minister's room. He didn't look his age. I resolved to time my next visit at vespers to hear what he had to say and sing. I shall not forget the experience. His devotions were long and very preachy. Then suddenly, he began to sing:

> My hope is built on nothing less
> than Jesus' blood and righteousness.

He had the most powerful ninety-year-old voice I had ever heard. When I left I thought—and still do—about a man at the end of his life, with only a bed and a bed stand, sharing his room with another, yet filling that whole building with his song of hope.

How's that for staying on the positive side!

Alas, some don't. We have considered the traps Satan uses to catch us, but we must remember we can't blame him for everything. At times we have no one to blame but ourselves. "Whoever digs a pit may fall into it" (Eccles. 10:8). We can fall into these pits late in life.

I had a friend who drove across the continent and back again. He drove thousands of miles in safety. He was almost home. Only three more miles to go. That's when he had his terrible accident. Sometimes the worst accidents happen closest to home. So, too, in the journey through life. After a lifetime of spiritual safety, we can run into trouble when we have almost reached that place which Jesus has prepared for us. Therefore, we must ask what we can do about those things that ensnare us and cause us to stumble in our later years.

Let us look again at the negatives we considered in the previous section.

Doubt

What can we do about doubt? This is certainly a matter for prayer. We must take doubt straight to Jesus. When we do this, we must be candid with him and say, as the man in the gospel story said, "Lord, I believe, help me to overcome my unbelief" (Mark 9:24).

146

*Are We Growing
Old Grumpily
and Negatively or
Gracefully and
Positively?*

When in the throes of doubt, we should read the Bible more, not less. If possible, we should reveal our spiritual problems to someone else. Pastors can help. We should also realize that not all questions have answers, and we must live with that. When we wonder about God's providential activity and cannot understand why this or that has happened, we must tell ourselves that the ways of heaven are inscrutable and past finding out. If we understood everything, we would be as great as God, with no need for faith.

Remember, too, faith needs to be exercised. If it is not, it will shrink and atrophy. We must remember the song "trust him—only trust him" and remind ourselves that his ways are higher, and that someday we'll understand. Am I speaking in cliches? I don't think so.

Another very practical thing for us to do when pondering doubt is to get busy, to put our minds on something else. It is good to let problems rest and come back to them later. This is no cop-out but good common sense. When we think so hard we can't think anymore, it's time to go fishing.

Self-esteem

If our negative is self-importance, we probably don't realize it. It makes us hard to live with. How blessed we are if someone tries in a kind way to open our eyes to this smudge on our face, so, as Robert Burns said, "You can see yourself as others see you." If our wives or husbands or perhaps someone else tells us we are acting self-important, we should not fly off the handle but rather ask ourselves if it's true.

When we stand under the stars, we can see how small we are. An astronaut in space looked out the window and saw our planet. He put his thumb on the window and couldn't see it anymore. His thumb was bigger than the earth. And the earth is so much bigger than we are. So we must shrink ourselves to normal size and develop a sense of humor. If someone tells us there is no one like us, instead of preening we should say, "And a good thing too. I don't think the Lord wants two of me."

148

*Are We Growing
Old Grumpily
and Negatively or
Gracefully and
Positively?*

On the other hand, those who have a low self-image need help as well. Psalm 8 says we have been made a little lower than the heavenly beings and crowned with glory and honor (Ps. 8:5). The fact that Jesus came to earth for us may not fill us with pride in ourselves. But it should give us proper self-respect.

Hypercriticism

Being hypercritical, we said, was also a negative. I fear it is not in short supply among us. Hypercriticism is found in all ages of life, but in ours more than most. It is a good thing to take special note that Jesus, in his Sermon on the Mount, singled this sin out. He said, "Why do you look at the speck of sawdust in your brother's eye and pay no attention to the plank in your own eye?" (Matt. 7:3). Jesus labeled this action hypocrisy (Matt. 7:5). The shoe fits, and we should wear it. Hypocrisy may keep us from having twenty-twenty vision with respect to someone else's little sins while being blind to our own big ones. The solution

for this sin is found in Psalm 139:23-24.
It is good to look it up.

Self-Pity

Self-pity is also one of our besetting
sins. It immobilizes those caught in its
mire. Whether our self-pity is brought
on by sorrow, loss, or other circumstances, its cure is found in the pages of
God's book. Those tending to feel sorry
for themselves do well to learn a lesson
from Psalms 42 and 43. "Why are you
downcast, O my soul? Why so dis-
turbed within me? Put your hope in
God."

Remember the doughnut we talked
about? Those who are filled with self-
pity are looking at the hole. However,
even in bad circumstances, we can still
count our blessings. It is good to focus
on them. An old anonymous proverb
says, "We have no right to ask, when
sorrow comes, 'Why did this happen to
me?' unless we ask the same question
for every joy that comes our way."

Our task is to drive the night away.
Eagles set their wings and use adverse
winds to soar higher. With God's help
we can do the same. I received a book

149

*Are We Growing
Old Grumpily
and Negatively or
Gracefully and
Positively?*

150

*Are We Growing
Old Grumpily
and Negatively or
Gracefully and
Positively?*

from my father on my seventeenth birthday. I wish I still had it. It was entitled, *Against Head Winds* and contained inspiring stories of some who had lived positive lives and made positive contributions despite the most negative circumstances.

Egocentricism

Earlier, we discussed the poison of self-centeredness. It is a universal phenomenon.

> Me and my wife,
> My son John and his wife,
> Us four and no more.

Such selfish thinking grows uglier with age. Its cure is to focus more, as is our Christian duty, on the needs of others. The lady I mentioned who had a prayer list of many names other than her own surely avoided this pitfall of age in which we become overly concerned with ourselves.

Retrospection

The forever-backward look some of us engage in is another negative that needs to be transformed into a positive. Those who are the Lord's should concentrate on the future. Jesus is coming again. No matter how old we are, our future is ever before us. Isaiah told the people in captivity to look ahead, not back. Those who wait on the Lord shall renew their strength for the onward journey. Onward Christian soldiers of whatever age. "I will come back," said Jesus (John 14:3). If much makes us look into the past, even more makes us, as Christians, look ahead.

Conservatism

Conservatism in the bad sense is also a sin of age. Surely, we ought to avoid being so set in our ways that our minds are closed and unchangeable. Surely, wisdom has not ended with our generation. Some of us need to open our minds—even if it takes a crowbar.

I recall an elderly saint who was totally opposed when our church council proposed leveling our old and venerated sanctuary and building a new one in its place. Given its weakened structure, it was necessary. However, the old man led the forces of opposition. At congregational meetings he spoke lengthily, eloquently, and lovingly of the

152

*Are We Growing
Old Grumpily
and Negatively or
Gracefully and
Positively?*

old sanctuary. It simply had to be preserved.

When the matter was finally put to vote after months of prayer and deliberation, the congregation voted to replace its sanctuary with a new one. Afterwards, all were called on to make a pledge. Those assigned to visit the elderly saint who had so vociferously opposed the new building project hesitated to make the call. They were sure they would not receive a kindly reception. Imagine their surprise and ours when they received not only a pledge but a very large one. After they expressed surprise, the man explained. The congregation had proceeded prayerfully. The matter had been weighed, and God had been asked to lead his people to a decision. Since he believed God had led, the old man was now ready not only to change his mind but also to support the building project with all his might.

Such behavior is atypical. But what an example for all of us oldsters whose minds are made up on everything!

To grow old gracefully, then, is to avoid all these pitfalls with God's help.

But there is more. As much as we are able, and with God's help, we must live a life of service.

The late William Eerdmans, founder of the internationally known William B. Eerdmans Publishing Company, was, to his dying day, impressed with Walter B. Alexander's story entitled, "Ninety-Six Bunches of Roses." In his old age Mr. Eerdmans told me it was a story that kept him young. In the story a minister called on a member of his church who had been ill. She had never been very active or highly visible. The minister saw her in the back row of Sunday services, but that was about all. He classified her as one on the fringes of church membership.

When the minister called on her, he found the conversation lagging. Looking through the window into her backyard, he noticed many roses. Searching for some conversational material, he commented on their beauty and, in the process, made a remarkable discovery. She said she was too old to do much anymore. But she loved roses and seemed to have a gift for growing them. She brought them to the local hospital

Are We Growing Old Grumpily and Negatively or Gracefully and Positively?

to cheer the sick. Just prior to her ill-ness, she had had a local boy deliver ninety-six bunches to the hospital.

The minister went home impressed with what he had learned. He had called on one of his older members. He had heard no complaints. Instead, he found a much more spiritually healthy Christian than he had expected to find, one whose life was focused on serving others. It makes me think of the words of St. Francis of Assisi: "Preach the gospel at all times. If necessary, use words." That was St. Francis' way of stressing the importance of concrete Christian service.

Not all of us can grow roses for hos-pital patients. Instead, some of us are hospital patients ourselves. And yet the secret of growing older gracefully is found in what we can do for God and for others.

After World War II the people in a German village tried to repair a statue of Christ that had been shattered by a bomb. They found all the pieces and lovingly put them together—all except the hands. They couldn't find the hands.

Later, someone hung a sign on the statue. It said, "I have no hands but yours."

How wonderful to look at our hands, gnarled now and touched by rheumatism, and know they can still be useful in the service of one whose hands were pierced for us. Ecclesiastes 9:10 makes no distinction between hands, old or young, busy or retired: "Whatever your hand finds to do, do it with all your might."

Ecclesiastes 7:17 asks, "Why die before your time?"

Some of us can use our hands in the service of others. Others of us can only fold them in prayer, like the ninety-year-old of whom I have written.

Are We Growing Old Grumpily and Negatively or Gracefully and Positively?

156

*Are We Growing
Old Grumpily
and Negatively or
Gracefully and
Positively?*

- In our thinking together about why some grow old gracefully and others do not, we made mention of Psalm 73. It is a Psalm of Asaph in which he wonders why the wicked prosper (Ps. 73:3).

- Some aged Christians have this same problem. They have earned God's "well done, good and faithful servant," but little else. Their lives have been beset with illness, poverty, and tragedy. Meanwhile, their godless neighbors have enjoyed good things in abundance. Thus, they tend to echo the words of Asaph, "In vain have I kept my heart pure . . . all day long I have been plagued" (Ps. 73:13-14). Thinking along these lines, they tend towards such negatives as doubt and self-pity.

- A preening evangelist came to town one day. He had just returned from Europe. I went to hear him with an elder from my church. The evangelist said he had appeared before the King of Norway. He said it was an event in his life that proved the truth of the

Bible when it says, "Seest thou a man diligent in his business? He shall stand before kings" (Prov. 22:29, KJV). Without turning my head too much, I looked at my elder with peripheral vision. He had been a faithful servant of the Lord. A pillar in the church. All his life he had eked out a meager existence running his small store. Despite his diligence, he had not gone very far. He had certainly never stood before kings. The evangelist had said something as insensitive as it was untrue. He had failed to show the other side of the coin: we are told that some who are diligent in their business come to stand before fiery furnaces (Dan. 3), while others come to stand alongside the author of Psalm 73.

Are We Growing Old Grumpily and Negatively or Gracefully and Positively?

- If the problem of Asaph is your problem too, notice the first four words of the psalm. Together they constitute a presupposition. Asaph is going to deal with a problem that disturbs him greatly. Yet before he does, he asserts his belief in the goodness of God. This is an important point that should not be missed. Asaph is not

158

*Are We Growing
Old Grumpily
and Negatively or
Gracefully and
Positively?*

going to see whether his reasoning will lead him either to the goodness or badness of God. Before he begins his wrestling, he posits his faith in God's goodness as something untouchable. This is a good point to make for those who, on the basis of what they observe, will determine the nature of God.

- Surely, verse 17 is important for all of us to notice. Asaph came to a fuller understanding when he entered the sanctuary. Often, going to church and hearing God's Word proclaimed will gain for the hearer the right perspective. The closing verses of this psalm entice us to go and do likewise. Look them up. Surely Psalm 73 is a rich mine for all, especially for those of us in the evening of life whose lot is less than we think it ought to be.

- As we consider Psalm 73, it is also good to review Lord's Day 10 of the Heidelberg Catechism. I must confess to times when I have wondered about its Q&A 27:

What do you understand by the providence of God?

Providence is
    the almighty and ever present
        power of God
    by which he upholds,
        as with his hand,
        heaven
        and earth
        and all creatures,
    and so rules them that
        leaf and blade,
        rain and drought,
        fruitful and lean years,
        food and drink,
        health and sickness,
        prosperity and poverty—
    all things, in fact, come to us
        not by chance
        but from his fatherly hand.

159

*Are We Growing
Old Grumpily
and Negatively or
Gracefully and
Positively?*

There is a problem here for many. It has surfaced in my mind, too, more than once. A senseless accident. A small child killed by a drunken driver. Does this happen "not by chance but by his fatherly hand"?

- I have discovered that older people often have a problem with this question and answer in the catechism. That is because we have seen and experienced more tragedies than

160

*Are We Growing
Old Grumpily
and Negatively or
Gracefully and
Positively?*

those who come after us. Some of us have buried a son or daughter. One of the hardest things in life for parents is to survive their children. Do these and other tragedies come through providence? Did it make any sense when God took your son or daughter whom your grandchildren needed so much, while he continues to uphold you, even though your work appears to be done?

- We deal with a mystery here. God's ways are unfathomable. At times we can only be still and know that God is God. In Ecclesiastes we are told there are times when wisdom dictates diligence (7:10). "Do not say, 'Why were the old days better than these?' For it is not wise to ask such questions." We must believe this in a profound way.

- In all of this, it is good to do what Asaph did—firmly fix your mind on the goodness of God before you wrestle with life's imponderables.

6

ARE WE AT THE BEGINNING OF THE END OR AT THE END OF THE BEGINNING?

It is appointed unto men once to die.

—Hebrews 9:27 [KJV]

165 ————————————
*Are We at the
Beginning of the
End or at the End
of the Beginning?*

END

*I*n the short story "The Man Who Met Death," Death and man hold a conversation. Knowing they would meet again someday, the man had a request. "I hate surprises," he said. "I wonder, therefore, whether it would be possible for you to give me some warning before you come to take me away." Death found this request not only understandable but reasonable as well, and so agreed. He would not drop in on the man suddenly, out of the blue. He would give him ample warning.

166
*Are We at the
Beginning of the
End or at the End
of the Beginning?*

"In fact," said Death, "I will give you not only one but several warnings."

Completely satisfied, the man went on his way. He put Death out of his mind. "Plenty of time to worry about it when I get a warning," he thought. Imagine his surprise a number of years later when Death suddenly appeared to take him away. "But this is not fair," said the man. "You gave me your word I would have ample warning, and now here you are, and you have given me none."

Death replied, "I have been true to my word. I have warned you more than once."

"But when?" replied the man. "When did you give me warning?"
"I gave you many," was the answer. "Remember your first gray hair? That was one of my first. Remember the day you discovered your hearing to be less acute? Then there was that visit to the doctor when he told you to slow down. Remember? I sent you shortness of breath quite a few times. And once, a small heart attack. Surely you remember that one!"

The man had to agree that death had given him many warnings.

Only—he had ignored them all.

We must take note of death's warning signs and realize they are harbingers of what lies ahead. Indeed, death comes sooner than we think. Time goes so quickly. The English priest Henry Twells wrote that for a small child, time crawls. For a young man, time walks. For the busy and working middle-aged, time runs. And for oldsters, time flies. Before we know it, death is at the door.

"So teach us to number our days," says Moses in Psalm 90. But how do we number them? As a child, by days. As growing boys and girls, by weeks and months. As adults, by years. And then, the older we get, by months again. Then, by weeks again. Finally, with death close by, by days once more.

Old is old, and it is prudent to acknowledge it. As Thomas Nashe wrote in his *Litany in Time of Plague*:

Beauty is but a flower
that wrinkles will devour.

Looking in the mirror, we see the wrinkles. We won't ever be young again,

168

*Are We at the
Beginning of the
End or at the End
of the Beginning?*

for time is irreversible. We use cosmetics. We comb our hair to cover the bald spot. Even so, we have passed age thirty-nine, although some of us won't admit it.

Did you ever see those fiftieth wedding anniversary pictures in the newspaper next to the wedding pictures of the same couples taken fifty years ago? Often, there seems to be no resemblance. Experts on the aging process say, however, that the older people become, the more they look like themselves. That is to say, their physical peculiarities become accentuated. The older we get the more we look like caricatures of our younger selves. At times, when I watch little children singing in the Christmas program, I see traces of their parents, even grandparents. I think I can tell what these children will look like when they reach threescore-and-ten.

Be that as it may, it isn't bad these days to be at the end of things. In many ways we have it much easier than our grandparents did. Think of the many churches and public buildings now barrier-free. The handicapped have special parking, and many places offer discounts for seniors.

We have special medicines and doctors, nurses and hospitals. Geriatrics is a science. We have pensions and social security. And there are more of us than ever before. Indeed, some people are beginning to consider us a drain on the economy. All the more reason for us to be pluses and not minuses wherever we can.

Some octogenarians attribute their longevity to not drinking or smoking, others to the fact that they are vegetarians. But such reasons are not taken too seriously by others who attribute their length of years to heredity or environment or both. Some people even credit tobacco and drink to their long stay among us. Yet, in the end, today's increasing life span can only be attributed to God, who has made available the knowledge about health and hygiene that has stretched our earthly sojourn. It is the Lord who is behind the graying of society and the church.

Along with added years, God has provided added conveniences. Ten fingers are not enough to count our many

Are We at the Beginning of the End or at the End of the Beginning?

blessings: beauty aids, false teeth, spectacles, contacts, radios, televisions, automobiles, retirement homes, rest homes, meals on wheels, hearing aids, telephones, miracle pills, total knee and hip replacements, and many spare body parts when we need them.

There is much more. God has given us roofs over our heads and food to eat. He has given us time to smell the flowers. In earlier years we were too busy to notice them. But now that he has slowed our walk, we notice the beauties of nature.

Above all God has given his Word. And himself. Those of us who are able can go to church. If we are homebound, we can hear sermons on radio or television. We also have books. And so we can grow in spiritual stature. God doesn't give us extra years without having a purpose for them. He says, "Continue to work out your salvation with fear and trembling, for it is God who works in you to will and to act according to his good purpose" (Phil. 2:12, 13).

The Lord tells us to make our calling and election sure (2 Pet. 1:10). What a blessing when he gives us time for these things! Surely, in age we must render to him that which Heidelberg Catechism Q&A 64 calls "the fruits of gratitude." How wonderful that we have a God who says to us, "Even to your old age and gray hairs I am he, I am he who will sustain you. I have made you and I will carry you" (Isa. 46:4).

We who are older have many blessings. Even advantages. For many of us it is a great time of life. But when all is said and done, we must not overlook that we are at the end. Ecclesiastes bluntly states, "There is a time to die" (Eccles. 3:2).

King Louis XIV of France once decreed the word "death" was never to be uttered in his presence. William Randolph Hearst, newspaper tycoon in more recent history, gave a similar order. Many older people have the same head-in-the-sand philosophy. I have sat with older couples more than once, one of whom was terminally ill. In their conversation together, they never spoke of death. I always found this sad. They could have used their moments to face the end together, to express their inmost feelings to each other. In sharing their

172

*Are We at the
Beginning of the
End or at the End
of the Beginning?*

deepest thoughts and fears, they could have enriched one another. Their tears might have commingled into a rich fountain. Instead, they shed them separately and in private, each intent on protecting the other. It is appointed unto each one of us to die, says the book of Hebrews, and who can face that better than the Christian?

Paul did not ignore the coming end. Instead, he used his last days to take inventory. He said, "I have fought the good fight, I have finished the race, I have kept the faith" (2 Tim. 4:7).

We, too, have largely finished the race. It is good then, at the end, to ask forgiveness for not having fought the fight as well as we should have, for not having kept the faith better than we did. Even so, the Lord will help us finish these last inches or years or miles, no matter how difficult they be.

In the summer Olympics of 1992, a runner from England pulled his hamstring muscle. I happened to be watching the event on television. He went down like a stone. Because it had happened to me years ago, I knew the race was over for him. He could not possibly finish the course. I'm sure he knew it too. Nevertheless, he tried to get up and take a step, only to fall down again.

Then an incredible thing happened. Someone came out of the stands of spectators and helped the stricken runner to his feet. I wondered who it was. The newspaper account on the following day revealed his identity—the father of the runner. He put his arms around his son, and together they headed for the finish line. They reached it long after the others had crossed. Yet Derek Redmond, for that was his name, finished the race with his father's help.

So it is with us. As Christians we do not fear death. Some of us may fear the process. It might be a bed of pain. It is good, therefore, to know our help is in the name of the Lord. We are like Derek Redmond. His father helped him finish the race. Our heavenly Father will help us do the same. As the closing words of Psalm 23 remind us, "Goodness and mercy will follow us," not just for awhile, but all our days.

He has also set eternity in the hearts of men.
—Ecclesiastes 3:11

— 174
*Are We at the
Beginning of the
End or at the End
of the Beginning?*

BEGINNING

For the Christian, old age, the beginning of the end, is really just the end of the beginning. After all, much more is to follow.

Throughout my years I often thought of buying a cottage. There was a time when I went shopping for one almost every summer. I never bought one, but I spent a lot of time dreaming. When cottage hunting, I noticed many cottages had names. I wondered what I would call my own. For awhile I sought more earnestly for a name than for a cottage itself. After considering many possibilities, I finally picked a name for my nonexistent cottage. I would call it "Postlude."

It seemed an appropriate designation for a cottage to which I might retire someday. After all, what could be more appropriate for a preacher? At the end of every Sunday service came the postlude. So, too, I reasoned, when I finished the active ministry and retired, there would be a "Postlude." It would be my cottage.

I told a friend about the name I had for a place that never was. His reaction was immediate. Instead of telling me how clever I was to have come up with such a name, he criticized my choice. He said I should have called it "Interlude"! "After all," he said, "when we come to the end of this life, there is the next." Of course, he was right. I was ashamed I had not thought of it myself. I changed the name of my nonexistent cottage from "Postlude" to "Interlude."

For us, more lies ahead than lies behind, even though what lies behind is a lot. Far before our births was a Paradise from which our first parents were excluded when they sinned. That resulted in death passing to us all (Rom. 5:12). But "God so loved the world that he gave his one and only Son, that whoever believes in him shall not perish but have eternal life" (John 3:16).

176

*Are We at the
Beginning of the
End or at the End
of the Beginning?*

Therefore, for us so much now lies ahead. In a New England cemetery is a gravestone that reads, "Death has overcome." Next to it is another, "Death is overcome." Because it is overcome, the Christian has life on both sides of the grave.

What we are told in the Bible we feel in our bones. As Ecclesiastes says, we have eternity in our hearts. Threescore-and-ten years are not enough to exhaust the potential that God has placed in all of us. In a lifetime of study, we scratch only the surface of knowledge. With inner eyes we can behold visions that rival sunsets in their beauty. Within our souls we can compose and hear (yet not bring to expression) such music as rivals Mozart. Though creatures of space, space cannot contain us; with our minds we can dwell upon the most distant star.

An organist friend of mine, now gone to glory, once said to me, "Only a fraction of what I feel comes through my fingers." The God who made her that way will let her produce music in the new earth such as she never could in this one.

On this earth we deal in minutes, hours, and days. Even ages. And yet we have minds that are not time bound. Poets understand this better than philosophers. John Milton did not dabble in time. Like the psalmist he reached beyond it. As someone observed, a friendship with the Eternal is an eternal friendship.

Within us are intimations of eternity that are verified by Scripture. Paul said, "For to me, to live is Christ but to die is gain" (Phil. 1:21). "No one living in Zion will say, 'I am ill'; and the sins of those who dwell there will be forgiven" (Isa. 33:24). Jesus said, "I will come back and take you to be with me that you also may be where I am" (John 14:3). The Bible contains many more references to the life everlasting.

By the sea of crystal
Saints in glory stand.

Before we can reach the other shore, however, we need to go through the valley of the shadow of death. It is important to notice that the Bible does not describe it as a mountaintop experience. It is a valley. The Bible is a realistic book.

178

*Are We at the
Beginning of the
End or at the End
of the Beginning?*

In 1 Corinthians 15:26 death is described as the last enemy. It is understandable, therefore, that many of us approach it with a measure of apprehension.

Surely, this is human, and God understands. It is important to ask the Lord to help us. Paul Sabatier tells a story about St. Francis who called for a stringed instrument when he was in pain, for praise is pain's antidote. I was reminded of that story when I went to call on a dying patient. As I approached her room, I could hear her singing softly, despite her pain. I paused outside the door and was deeply moved. The hymn was a familiar one:

> Precious Lord, take my hand,
> lead me on, help me stand;
> I am tired, I am weak, I am worn;
> through the storm, through the night,
> lead me on to the light;
> take my hand, precious Lord,
> lead me home.

Perhaps she knew the second verse, too, although she did not sing it.

> When my way grows drear,
> precious Lord, linger near;
> when my life is almost gone,

hear my cry, hear my call,
hold my hand, lest I fall;
take my hand, precious Lord,
lead me home.

179

*Are We at the
Beginning of the
End or at the End
of the Beginning?*

Surely, we may trust that he will take us by the hand and lead us through the valley of the shadow. When we are apprehensive, it may help to know we are not alone. John Bunyan, in *Pilgrim's Progress*, tells us that when Christian's wife received a letter saying she would die, she stepped calmly into the river of death without fear. But when Christian made the same journey, he was almost overcome. Even so, both reached the other side. We may be assured that "he will be our guide even unto the end" (Ps. 48:14). Having the assurance that Jesus will go with us, even through our last days, we may focus on what lies ahead (Matt. 28:20).

In this connection we must understand what death is for the Christian. Heidelberg Catechism Q&A 42 tells us, "Our death does not pay the debts of our sins. Rather, it puts an end to our sinning and is our entrance into eternal life." For this reason Paul felt such a desire to depart and be with Christ

180

Are We at the
Beginning of the
End or at the End
of the Beginning?

(Phil. 1:23). If death is a tunnel, as some describe it, we must see the great light at the end. We can believe that "in all things [our deaths, too] God works for the good of those who love him" (Rom. 8:28). Those who cannot say this and who do not know him should be grateful time remains to come to him in penitence and love, for "now is the day of salvation" (2 Cor. 6:2).

If old age for the Christian is only the end of the beginning, it is good to set our houses in order. When King Hezekiah was ill and at the point of death, the prophet went to him and said, "This is what the Lord says, 'put your house in order because you are going to die' " (2 Kings 20:1). To Hezekiah's advantage he was given this notification. He was given opportunity to arrange his affairs.

Our gray hairs and failing strength give us notification as well. We are careless, therefore, if we do not tend to what needs tending to, both spiritually and materially. Good stewardship demands that we make arrangements, through wills or other means, for that which the Lord has entrusted to our care.

Unlike Hezekiah, many receive no notification. They are suddenly snatched away. One moment they are here, the next they are gone. It is good, therefore, for all Christians to have their houses in order all the time; we never know what a day will bring. But for those of us who have been given notice, we who are up in years, there is no excuse for not being ready when God calls us into his marvelous light.

Zechariah 14:7 contains a statement I would like to appropriate for our thinking about age. There we read, "When evening comes, there will be light." The prophet is speaking of the Lord's coming and reigning over all. Forgive me for taking this wonderful sentence out of context and making it apply to Christian old age.

The world sees old people as being over the hill or at the end of their ropes. We are on a downward course. Aristotle equated age with degeneration on all fronts. If we were physical beings and nothing more, there might be something to say for this worldly view. But we are soul and body, made in God's image. Because we are up in years does

182

Are We at the
Beginning of the
End or at the End
of the Beginning?

not mean we are down on the graph of life. Instead of being on the far side of a bell curve, we are ever rising, rising, rising. And so, at evening it will be light.

This is not the order of nature. In the natural ordering of the day, evening is dark. It is then that the shadows lengthen, and the darkness deepens. But the order of grace is the reverse. The sun never stops climbing. At evening the light is brighter than ever. God saves the best for last. Tennyson wrote:

> Twilight and evening bell
> And after that the dark.

But for the Christian, full of years, it will be light at evening. As Paul wrote to the Thessalonians, "You are all sons of the light and sons of the day. We do not belong to the night or to the darkness" (1 Thess. 5:5).

We are not at the beginning of the end. We are only at the end of the beginning. There is much more to come.

REFLECTIONS

183

*Are We at the
Beginning of the
End or at the End
of the Beginning?*

- John 14 is often described as the Bible's most comforting chapter. It is a fine passage to contemplate. In it we find:

  A person: verse 1
  A place: verse 2
  A path: verse 6

  And the person is the path to the place.

- We have noted that even in old age we are still on the growing edge. As Paul says, we are the children of the light. Many other passages in the Bible lend weight to the thought that in old age we are not spent and at the end: "Your youth is renewed like the eagle's" (Ps. 103:5). A favorite of many is the closing verse of Isaiah 40:31: "Those who hope in the Lord will renew their strength. They will soar on wings like eagles; they will run and not grow weary, they will walk and not be faint." Can you find similar passages in Scripture?

- Paul was not a young man when he set out on his first missionary journey. It is entirely reasonable to suspect the hardships of travel and

184

*Are We at the
Beginning of the
End or at the End
of the Beginning?*

persecution also took their toll because of his age. Nevertheless, he could write to the Philippians, "I have learned to be content whatever the circumstances." This brought him a serenity we too should have when we tend to complain about our physical hardships.

- Then, too, Paul had that thorn in the flesh of which he wrote in 2 Corinthians 12. The Lord did not relieve him of it—whatever it was—but said, " 'My grace is sufficient for you' " (2 Cor. 12:9). After that Paul ceased asking the Lord for relief.

- This story contains a lesson for those of us who keep badgering the Lord for relief. This is not to say we may not "cast all our cares on him," but we may do so only with the belief that whatever he will do or not do about them is best, for "he cares for you."

- There is a beautiful expression of faith and trust for those who feel that God is not helping them in their old age. I have used it often to reassure some aged saint. It is found in Psalm 18:36: "You broaden the path beneath

me, so that my ankles do not turn."
Think about it.

- The Bible is for people of every age, including those of us in the evening of life. It is a lamp to our feet and a light upon our path (Ps. 119:105). Here is the Word:

185
*Are We at the
Beginning of the
End or at the End
of the Beginning?*

—*for those disappointed in the way things turned out:*
I know, O Lord, that a man's life is not his own; it is not for man to direct his steps. Correct me, Lord, but only with justice—not in your anger, lest you reduce me to nothing (Jer. 10:23, 24).

—*for those facing uncertainty:*
So do not fear, for I am with you; do not be dismayed, for I am your God. I will strengthen you and help you; I will uphold you with my righteous right hand (Isa. 41:10).

—*for those who need reassurance:*
But now, this is what the Lord says—he who created you, O Jacob, he who formed you, O Israel; "Fear not, for I have redeemed you; I have summoned you by name; you are mine. When you pass through the waters, I will be with you; and when you pass

through the rivers, they will not sweep over you. When you walk through the fire, you will not be burned; the flames will not set you ablaze" (Isa. 43:1, 2).

—*for those who have suffered material loss:* Though the fig tree does not bud and there are no grapes on the vines, though the olive crop fails and the fields produce no food, though there are no sheep in the pen and no cattle in the stalls, yet I will rejoice in the Lord, I will be joyful in God my Savior (Hab. 3:17, 18).

—*for those who wonder about God's providential ways:* For I am convinced that neither death nor life, neither angels nor demons, neither the present nor the future, nor any powers, neither height or depth, nor anything else in all creation, will be able to separate us from the love of God that is in Christ Jesus our Lord (Rom. 8:38, 39).

Can you supply other passages? I'll leave you some space.

187

*Are We at the
Beginning of the
End or at the End
of the Beginning?*

- In 1 Corinthians 15:26 Paul speaks of death as the last enemy. Through the resurrection of Christ this enemy has been overcome. Even so, death is still an enemy. In Philippians 1:21, Paul shows no fear of this enemy when he speaks of his death as gain. In verse 23 he again shows no fear when he speaks of longing to depart and be with Christ.

- In 2 Corinthians 5, however, we see another side of Paul. There he speaks in the first verse about our earthly tent which will be destroyed. We will then have a building of God, eternal in the heavens. Paul has no doubt about this. We might expect he would comment on this truth with a hallelu-jah or two. Instead, we hear a groan. He says in verse 4 that while we are in this tent we are burdened because we do not want to be unclothed.

- How do you read this passage? If I read it correctly, I see a Paul who, on the one hand, is not afraid of the last

188

Are We at the
Beginning of the
End or at the End
of the Beginning?

enemy ("O death, where is your sting?" [1 Cor. 15:55]). On the other hand, he views death with apprehension (2 Cor. 5:4). If this is a true reading, we can be comforted by it. If so great a Christian as Paul could show his humanness here, then we can show ours as well.

Goodbye

(GOD BE WITH YOU)

t was in the fall. Two leaves in a tree were holding on for dear life. So many of their fellow leaves had disappeared. They had fallen and been blown away. One leaf said to the other, "I wonder what it's like to be removed from your place."

The other replied, "I don't know. Not a single leaf has ever returned to tell us."

So it is with us. We bury our dead and wonder what it's like. What is heaven like? Not a single one has ever come back to tell us.

Heaven is so completely other that no language can describe it in a way that tiny minds can grasp. Thus, the Bible speaks to us about heaven only in terms of what is not there (Rev. 21-22). But it does tell us who is there—our Lord! This is sufficient.

Long ago I heard a story I find helpful. A doctor had an office adjoining his house. His dog was trained never to enter his office even if the door was open. One day a patient whose death was imminent came to see the doctor. Since both were Christians, the conversation drifted to a discussion of the hereafter. The patient expressed some apprehensions. "I don't know what it's like up there," he said.

"Neither do I," said the doctor. Then he had an idea. He told his patient he had a dog that had been trained never to enter his office even if the door was open. "But now," said the doctor, "I'm going to call him in."

The doctor opened the door. He returned to his chair behind his desk. He called the dog, who appeared in the doorway but, being trained, did not enter the office. The doctor called, urged, and encouraged the animal to cross the threshold. Finally, the dog could resist no longer and with a few giant leaps landed happily in his master's lap.

The doctor turned to his patient and said, "For a Christian, dying is like that. It is going where you have never been before. But it's all right because the Master is there."

Goodbye! (This expression is a contraction of "God be with you.")

God be with you.
Till we meet again.

AS LONG AS I LIVE

THOUGHTS ON GROWING OLDER

Jacob D. Eppinga

DISCUSSION GUIDE

1

ARE OUR SENIOR YEARS A BANE
OR A BLESSING?

Opening

If possible, schedule an introductory session in which the group leader and group members introduce themselves and obtain copies of *As Long As I Live.* Group members would have a better grasp of Ecclesiastes 12, the focal point of Eppinga's first chapter, if they read the entire book of Ecclesiastes before the next meeting.

Begin your first regular meeting by reading Ecclesiastes 12 responsively. Pray that God will help all group members to live fruitful lives in which they remember their Creator, not only in the days of their youth but all the days of their lives.

For Discussion

For all chapters please select the questions and activities that best fit the time you have and the interests of your group members.

1. React to this statement: "Many people consider Ecclesiastes the most depressing book they have ever read."

a. Does the repetition of these words: "Meaningless! Meaningless! Everything is meaningless" suggest that the writer sees no good or meaning in life? How else do you interpret these words?

b. Do you see any hope in the book? If so, where, and what is hopeful about it?

c. As a group read "The Conclusion of the Matter"(Eccl. 12:9-14). Does this section give a new or different slant to Ecclesiastes?

2. Eppinga speaks of the many "banes" of old age, including a number of physical problems. Without going into too many details, talk about some of the physical limitations you've experienced and their impact on your life.

3. Old age brings emotional struggles as well as physical problems. Discuss together what you believe is the older person's major emotional struggle. Is it facing death? Is it the loss of physical strength and beauty or mental acuity? Both young and old should respond to this question.

4. In Eastern cultures old age is welcomed; the old are honored for their wisdom. The biblical portrait of the elderly is colored by honor and glory as well (read 1 Chron. 29:28 and Prov. 16:31).

a. What information do you have that indicates how other cultures view old age and treat the aged? Compare and contrast with the treatment of the elderly in Western culture.

b. Why is age viewed so differently in Western culture?

c. Does our treatment of the elderly reflect other aspects of our culture?

d. Relate these questions to Eppinga's statement in "Reflections": "A people who honor their elders have a future."

5. Chapter 1 talks about civilization's unbelievable progress (eg., the advent of computers).

a. Discuss some other changes that have occurred in our society since the thirties and forties.

b. What are some of the older group members' reactions to these changes? What disturbs you about today's culture? What, if anything, is better in today's world?

c. Older group members may want to describe life in years past. What occupations no longer exist today? How is entertainment different?

6. Eppinga says, "The winter of life has rewards and beauties peculiarly its own." Respond to that statement.

Can you add to the rewards and beauties that Eppinga mentions? Why then do we treat old age so negatively?

7. Reflect again on the ninety-year-old woman's response to Eppinga's question about which decade in life she considered best. What decade in life do each of you see as best? Why?

8. In several paragraphs in his "Reflections" section, Eppinga asks, "What is a good old age?" Discuss this question, having each group member give his or her response. Would anyone really desire to reach the age Jacob did as described in Genesis 47?

Closing

Read the familiar verses of Ecclesiastes 3:1-8 which begin, "There is a time for everything, and a season for every activity under heaven." Then offer sentence prayers, each of you counting the blessings of your life and asking God for aid in times of hardship and illness.

2

ARE WE GROWING OLD OR GROWING UP?

Opening

Read Psalm 92, which contains a good description of healthy old age (see v. 12-15). You may want to say the last verse of this psalm in unison as a prayer of praise and testimony: "The Lord is upright; he is my Rock; and there is no wickedness in him."

For Discussion

Please select the questions and activities that best fit the time you have and the interests of your group members.

1. Discuss the tendency of some older people to try to appear and act much younger than they are.
    a. Is their behavior a way of striking back at the younger generation for poor treatment?
    b. How much is self-esteem involved?
    c. How much is denial involved? React to this statement: "Denial, in moderation, is a useful tool for maintaining a sense of stability. If carried too far, it can be haz-

ardous" (Sell, *Transitions Through Adult Life*, p. 225).

2. Retirement is probably the most crucial life change for the older adult. Break into groups of three to five people to discuss the following questions about retirement. After a brief time for small group discussion, the large group may discuss the problems and joys of retirement with input from each of the smaller groups.

   a. Eppinga speaks of the traditional wife's adjustment to having her husband "underfoot." What other adjustments and challenges occur with retirement?

   b. How do they differ for men and for women?

   c. What opportunities are available for those in retirement?

   d. How can someone prepare for retirement—both practically and psychologically?

   e. What can the church do to help people cope with retirement?

3. Proverbs 20:29 says "gray hair [is] the splendor of the old." For Eppinga one of the splendors is that older people have come to a truer understanding of God's grace and mercy in their lives. How do you understand this passage? What

might you add to Eppinga's perception of the splendor of being old?

4. Eppinga says spiritual growth is a long, slow process with frequent backtracking.

   a. Note his comments in "Reflections" about the process of sanctification. Do some people actually reach true sainthood in this life? What does that mean?

   b. What about those Christians (like Eppinga's aged parishioner) who reach old age and yet are plagued with doubt about eternal life and the resurrection? Have they not grown spiritually? How does doubt fit into spiritual maturity?

5. How do we cultivate and nurture the fruits of the Spirit? What kind of fruit can we bear in old age? (Read together Ps. 92:12-15). How do you understand the psalmist's words— "So teach us to number our days"? What does Eppinga mean when he says that work is implied in those words?

6. Discuss guilt in the Christian life. The modern psychologist would probably say that all guilt is detrimental to people's psyches. Do you think that is true? Can you think of some useful functions of guilt?

7. Discuss ways the Lord nourishes us spiritually.

a. What are our obligations in the light of God's nourishment?

b. When life brings its inevitable trials and tribulations, what should our attitude be?

c. Eppinga wonders how some can be "so negative" in the light of God's nourishment and care. But how is it possible to remain positive when life is one trial after another?

Closing

Sing "Spirit of God, Who Dwells Within My Heart" (#419, *Psalter Hymnal*; #326, *Presbyterian Hymnal*; #445, *Rejoice in the Lord*; #338, *Trinity Hymnal*). Group members could also pair off and pray for each other, asking God to bless one another with a fruitful and long life.

3

CAN OUR LOSSES BE TURNED INTO GAINS?

Opening

For your opening prayer, divide into two groups and read Psalm 71 responsively.

For Discussion

Please select the questions and activities that best fit the time you have and the interests of your group members.

1. Spend some time talking about the losses of old age, using some or all of the questions below. If your group is large, divide into smaller groups for better discussion.

   a. React to Eppinga's list of losses. Which others can you add?

   b. What losses that come with age does David describe in Psalm 71.

   c. What do you believe are the most difficult or poignant losses? How did they or would they affect you?

   d. In *Ministry with Aging*, John Bennet writes, "Society's stereotypes of the elderly as people who are unhealthy, ingrown, inactive, out-of-date in their ideas, rigid, and vulnerable to 'senility,' often have the effect of self-fulfilling prophecies" (*Transitions Through Adult Life*, p. 203).

Eppinga touches on the same idea when he says, "Not only do you reckon your age in terms of losses. Others do, too." Please react to this statement. If you are elderly, how have others' views of you and your abilities affected your view of yourself? Have you had a demeaning experience like the one Eppinga describes with the nurse? If so, how did it make you feel? How do you maintain your dignity in these kinds of situations?

e. How can the church influence people's perspectives of old age?

f. Are loneliness, boredom, and idleness a problem for any of the elderly in the group? What are some good ways to combat these problems?

2. It would give the group a new and different perspective on the losses of age if, before this session, a group member could visit a friend or loved one confined in a rest home and conduct a short interview of that person on tape. If this has occurred,

play the tape and discuss the confined person's perspective of the losses that come with age. How are they the same or different from the perspectives of those in the group?

3. Respond to Eppinga's "hints" concerning ways and means to keep losses in perspective. They are: (1) to take care of one's health; (2) to accept the signs of old age; (3) to ignore others' judgments; (4) to give the next generation room to grow and develop in its own way; (5) to read God's Word.
   a. Are these hints helpful? How?
   b. What might you add to the list?
   c. How have the elderly in the group kept their losses in perspective?
4. Spend some time talking about the gains of old age, using some or all of the questions below. Once again, if your group is large, divide into smaller groups for better discussion.
   a. Draw on Chapter 3 and the experiences of group members to list some of the gains or "good things" about getting older.
   b. Take another look at Psalm 71, this time noting some of the "good things" it states or implies about old age.
   c. Are there any "good things" for people confined in rest homes? Please comment.

d. What are some meaningful duties and activities the elderly can be involved in to remain useful and productive?

5. Eppinga mentions grandparenting as one of the pluses of old age. For those grandparents in the group:

   a. What is expected of you as a grandparent?

   b. Do you think that is too much? Too little?

   c. What contributions do you or can you make to your grandchildren?

Closing

Reflect again on the gains and losses of old age. Close the session with sentence prayers in which group members are invited to ask God's help in accepting specific losses of old age and to praise God for specific blessings or gains. You may also want to sing, "What a Friend We Have in Jesus" (#579, *Psalter Hymnal*; #403, *Presbyterian Hymnal*; #507, *Rejoice in the Lord*; #629, *Trinity Hymnal*).

4

CAN WORRY ADD A SINGLE HOUR TO OUR LIVES?

Opening

Begin by reminding the group that this lesson is on worry and trust. Read Matthew 6:25-34 in unison, and then sing, "When We Walk with the Lord" (#548, *Psalter Hymnal*; #672, *Trinity Hymnal*), which has "Trust and Obey" as its refrain.

For Discussion

Please select the questions and activities that best fit the time you have and the interests of your group members.

1. Eppinga lists the worries of old age: worries about health, money, the future, getting Alzheimer's disease, and death.
   a. What can you add to the list?
   b. What is most worrisome for you about old age?
   c. Do any of you know someone like Mabel whose world is filled with worry and complaint? How do you respond to these people? Do you agree that there is a little bit

of Mabel in all of us? What can we do about that?

d. If we are inclined to be worriers, how is it possible to escape from this mindset?

e. In "Reflections" Eppinga says Philippians 4:16 has helped him in his struggle against worry. What Bible passages have been helpful to you in this regard?

2. Pair a younger or middle-aged person with an older person in the group to compare the worries of different age groups. Consider these questions: How are your worries alike? How do they differ? How does each person deal with these worries? Report back to the large group.

3. Do some group members live in retirement homes? If so, use this time to talk about the transition from their homes to the retirement homes.

a. What was difficult? What was easy?

b. What are the benefits and/or drawbacks of retirement-home living?

d. Did your children urge the move, or was it your idea? How did this factor affect your perspective on the move?

4. Eppinga only touches on the fear of death, but that is a major fear for all ages. With the fear of death comes many other worries: for example, people may worry about their wills or about the nature of their death. Make a list of these worries and talk together about how each of you deal with them.

5. Jesus says, "Do not worry about tomorrow, for tomorrow will worry about itself. Each day has enough trouble of its own" (Matt. 6:34). He is telling us to live one day at a time. What does that mean to you? Is it really possible for any of us to live this way? Why do we prefer to live in the past or the future?

6. "There must be a reason for getting up in the morning. Our lives still need purpose," says Eppinga about retired persons. Please react to this statement. What is your reason for getting up in the morning?

Closing

Read together these verses from Isaiah 43:

This is what the Lord says—he who created you, O Jacob, he who formed you, O Israel; "Fear not, for I have redeemed you; I have summoned you by name; you are mine. When you pass through the waters I will be with you; and when you pass through the rivers, they will not sweep over you. When you walk through the fire, you will not be burned; the flames will not set you ablaze. For I am the Lord, your God, the Holy one of Israel, your Savior.

Close with a time of silent, personal prayer in which each participant brings his or her worries to God. Begin with these words: "Dear God, These are my worries. . . . If possible, please provide a cure for my cares. But in all things, help me to trust and obey your will."

5

ARE WE GROWING OLD GRUMPILY AND NEGATIVELY OR GRACEFULLY AND POSITIVELY?

Opening

Divide into two groups, then read responsively Psalm 73, the psalm of Asaph, to which Eppinga refers in "Reflections." Pray that God may help us to grow old gracefully, to see the bright side of our world, and to go through life with a song on our lips.

For Discussion

Please select the questions and activities that best fit the time you have and the interests of your group members.

1. Look more closely at Psalm 73. Eppinga says it is "a rich mine for all, especially for those in the evening of life whose lot is less than [they] think it ought to be."
   a. What verses are particularly comforting for those whose lives haven't been a "bed of roses"?
   b. Asaph admits to envy of the wicked who prosper (verse 3). Do you sometimes find yourself

falling into the same trap? Does this envy result in negative thoughts and feelings?

c. Asaph seems to find comfort in the fact that the wicked who prosper on earth will eventually be relegated to the terrors of hell. What do you think of this?

d. How does this psalm relate to having a positive attitude in old age?

2. Eppinga says, "Young people need to know how to live so their old age will be a melody and not a dirge." How can younger people prepare themselves for old age? How can the way they live now ensure a happy, rather than crotchety, old age?

3. Look at Eppinga's list of the bad habits or sins of old age: self-importance, egocentrism, overdependence, self-pity, hypercriticism, retrospection, conservatism.

a. Are they problems for people of all ages? Why?

b. Which ones are particular problems for the aged?

c. Eppinga says "we ought to avoid being so set in our ways that our minds are closed and unchangeable." Have you ever changed your mind about some church issue you felt strongly about? What changed your mind? (See the story of the aged parishioner who opposed the church building project.)

  e. React to this statement: Reminiscing, or retrospection, is not a bad habit of old age but is instead "a sign of health and should be encouraged" (Sell, *Transitions Through Adult Life*, pp.224-225).

4. Eppinga also talks about the problem of doubt for the elderly.

  a. He makes special mention of doubt concerning the doctrine of providence. People wonder: If God is in control, why do so many bad things happen to so many good people? Why is this especially a concern for the elderly? What Bible passages comfort you when pondering this problem?

  b. Eppinga says some people experience more serious doubt—about the truth of the Bible and the existence of God. (Is it all a "giant fairy tale after all?") Do you think only "some" people experience this doubt? In what circumstances might such questions arise?

  c. When C. S. Lewis reflects on the death of his wife, he, too, finds himself doubting. But he says that he didn't think he was in danger "of ceasing to believe in God." He felt, instead, "The real danger is of coming to believe such dreadful things about Him" (*A Grief Observed*). Have you felt this way when facing such traumas as the death of someone close to you? How have you dealt with this kind of doubt?

5. Eppinga balances his "Negative" section with a "Positive" one. In it he takes each of the sins or pitfalls mentioned in the earlier section and gives advice about how to deal with them in a positive manner.

   a. He tells us to deal with our doubt by praying, by speaking to someone else, perhaps a pastor; by reminding ourselves that the ways of God are beyond knowing; and by keeping busy with the practical aspects of life. Do you think this is helpful advice? What other hints may you have about dealing with doubt?

   b. Eppinga says the solution for the sin of hypercriticism is found in Psalm 139:23-24. Read these verses. How is this a solution? Put these words into practical, everyday language.

   c. What means or methods do you use to avoid self-pity? How can we help others in this regard?

6. Eppinga stresses that to remain positive in old age we must live lives of

service to God. Some service is highly visible. But think of all the quiet ways people serve others—like the woman in "Ninety-Six Bunches of Roses." Share with the group the various quiet services you may have received from others.

Chapter 5

Closing

Each member of the group may pray silently. Use the following words as an opener to the prayer: "Dear God, we know your ways are unfathomable. Help us to be still and know that you are God. Help us, too, in all life's mysteries and trials to count these our blessings. . . . "

6

ARE WE AT THE BEGINNING OF
THE END OR AT THE END OF THE
BEGINNING?

Opening

Read together John 14:1-27. The leader may want to read the words of Jesus and assign others in the group the words of Thomas, Philip, and Judas (not Judas Iscariot).

For Discussion

Please select the questions and activities that best fit the time you have and the interests of your group members.

1. Reflect on Eppinga's statement: "Time goes so quickly." As Eppinga describes it in this chapter, is English priest Henry Twells' analysis of the passing of time at different ages an accurate one? Various group members of different ages might want to react to this question. Does time fly mainly for those in middle and old age?

2. The Bible says death is the last enemy we must overcome. It is

understandable that many of us approach it with apprehension.

a. What apprehensions do the older members of your group have?

b. Look up 2 Corinthians 5:4. Do you think Paul shows apprehension about death here?

c. How does facing your own death differ from facing the death of a spouse, a child, or a friend?

d. Eppinga mentions the hymn that was a comfort to a dying parishioner: "Precious Lord, Take My Hand." What hymns or Bible verses are a comfort to you?

e. When both C. S. Lewis and Nicholas Wolterstorff faced the death of a loved one (for Lewis, his wife; for Wolterstorff, his son), they felt the absence of God. Lewis says, "Meanwhile, where is God? This is one of the most disquieting symptoms" (*A Grief Observed*, p. 4). Wolterstorff says, "[God] hides. His face he does not show us" (*Lament for a Son*, p. 75). Have you experienced this absence of God in the same circumstances? Is this the feeling people are expressing when they face the imminent death of a loved one and say, "I can't pray"? What, if anything, can we do to dispel the doubts that arise at these times?

e. Practically speaking, how should we get our "houses" in order before we die?

3. Eppinga says, "It isn't all that bad these days to be at the end of things." Do you agree with that statement? Do we have it much better than our grandparents did? What can you add to his list of things that are better today? In what ways might our grandparents have had it better when they faced the end of life?

4. Eppinga's title for chapter 6 is a twist on some of the words from T. S. Eliot's *Four Quartets*. Note these two passages:

What we call the beginning is often the end
And to make an end is to make a beginning.

. . . .

We shall not cease from exploration
And the end of all our exploring
Will be to arrive where we started
And know the place for the first time.

. . . .

A condition of complete simplicity
(Costing not less than everything)
—"Little Gidding" V

. . . We must be still and still moving
Into another intensity
For a further union, a deeper
    communion
Through the dark cold and the
    empty desolation,
The wave cry, the wind cry,
    the vast waters
Of the petrel and the porpoise.
    In my end is my beginning.
           —"East Coker" V

How does this metaphorical language relate to chapter 6? Remember, Eliot was a Christian when he wrote these words. Can you relate some of these lines to biblical passages and injunctions—for example, "Costing not less than everything," "We must be still," "A deeper communion," "Through the dark cold"? How does this poetic language enhance your understanding of Eppinga's words about beginnings and endings?

5. Read aloud Eppinga's "Goodbye" section. Is his story helpful? What do you find helpful when contemplating life beyond this life? What do you think life in the "new earth" will be like?

Closing:
    Close with this prayer:

Dear God, Thank you for broadening the path beneath us so that our ankles do not turn. When we do stumble and fall and become afraid, help us to listen to Jesus' words of assurance: "Peace I leave with you; my peace I give you. I do not give to you as the world gives. Do not let your hearts be troubled and do not be afraid." May we always trust in you and so find in our ends, our beginning. In Jesus' name we pray, Amen.

You may also want to sing, "God Be with You Till We Meet Again" (#316, *Psalter Hymnal*; #540, *Presbyterian Hymnal*; #445, *Rejoice in the Lord*; #338, *Trinity Hymnal*).